the Ego-Less SELF

Achieving Peace & Tranquility Beyond All Understanding

Cardwell C. Nuckols, Ph.D.

Health Communications, Inc.
Deerfield Beach, Florida

www.hcibooks.com

Library of Congress Cataloging-in-Publication Data

Nuckols, Cardwell C.
   The ego-less self : achieving peace & tranquility beyond all
understanding / Cardwell C. Nuckols.
      p. cm.
   ISBN-13: 978-0-7573-1541-1
   ISBN-10: 0-7573-1541-0
   1. Ego (Psychology)   2. Spirituality.   3. Happiness.   I. Title.
   BF175.5.E35N83 2010
   204'.4—dc22

                                                          2010023665

Publisher: Health Communications, Inc.
         3201 S.W. 15th Street
         Deerfield Beach, FL 33442–8190

Cover design by Larissa Hise Henoch
Interior design and formatting by Dawn Von Strolley Grove

I dedicate this book to God,
who is solely responsible for all that I am
and all that I may become.
Thank you for speaking through me.

Do not care
overly much for
wealth or power or fame
or one day you will meet someone
who cares for none of these things
and you might realize
how poor you have become.

—Rudyard Kipling (1865–1936)

Contents

Acknowledgments

To my son Camden, not only because he is my son, but because of what he has become as a young man.

To my friends Chuck and Taina Broes for their friendship, understanding, and always a place to stay.

To my friends John McAndrew and Judi Bixby. A friend is the highest accolade I know.

To my friend Sid Farrar, a fellow pilgrim on the path, whose honesty, integrity, and encouragement are always very much appreciated.

To my friend Siobhan Morse for her deep sense of service and for her help with this book.

A Note About Religion, Spiritual Traditions, and Language

During my spiritual journey throughout this lifetime, I have explored many different religions and spiritual traditions, and I have taken various paths within these religions and traditions. However, I have learned that it is best to find one path and deeply immerse oneself in the teachings of that path as opposed to horizontally flipping back and forth between religions or traditions. Contemplative Christianity—an early Christian mystical movement—served as a fulcrum point that permitted me to balance some of the contemplative and meditative traditions of Buddhism and Hinduism with the nonlinear teachings of Christianity, particularly the teachings of Jesus Christ. It is this contemplative Christian influence that is infused into this work.

There are many words that are used in reference to God. Although this book is written from a contemplative Christian perspective, I have tried to be inclusive of other religions or spiritual paths. Moreover, when I refer to God throughout this book, I am referring to the God of my understanding, so please feel free to replace this word with your word of choice, such as "Higher Power," "God of my understanding," or whatever word or concept works for you. I also rely on the teachings of Jesus throughout the book to illustrate some spiritual concepts. Jesus was a wise, enlightened teacher, and you do not have to be Christian to benefit from his teachings.

Also, please understand that the language of the spiritual world is subjective, and at times the concepts are hard to capture in words. For example, the linear world of physicality that we live in is understandable to us. We see it, hear it, smell it, taste it, and touch it. It is what we have grown up to understand as reality. The subjective, nonlinear world is fluid. It presents itself on many levels that are not immediately available to us. I have done my best to communicate with you throughout this book on nonlinear, spiritual matters. If a concept is difficult to grasp, try approaching it from a different angle or just sit with it for a time and allow the meaning to come to you.

Introduction

A human being is a part of a whole, called by us the universe, a part limited in time and space. He experiences himself, his thoughts and feelings as something separated from the rest . . . a kind of optical delusion of his consciousness. This delusion is a kind of prison for us, restricting us to our personal desires and to affection for a few persons nearest to us. Our task must be to free ourselves from this prison by widening our circle of compassion to embrace all living creatures and the whole of nature in its beauty.

—Albert Einstein

Begin by knowing that spiritual experiences are subjective and don't use a strict scientific paradigm and thus lack formal objectivity. According to nonlinear physics, there seems to be no such thing as formal scientific objectivity anyway. The pioneers of nonlinear physics were rather startled by their discovery that we are all intrinsically connected, and they turned to philosophy and the spiritual world to explain their findings. Wolfgang Pauli turned to archetypes and the Kabbalah, Niels Bohr to the Tao and Chinese philosophy, Erwin Schrödinger to Hindu philosophy, and Werner Heisenberg to the platonic theory of ancient Greece to understand that we cannot separate ourselves from our surroundings. We are not stand-alone entities; we are in constant interaction with the energy surrounding us. We are continuously emitting and receiving biophotons (light radiated from the cells of all living things) from our surroundings. We are connected to everything and can never be alone. Our mere presence changes the world around us for better or for worse.

Heisenberg's uncertainty principle tells us that any attempt to observe an electron alters it. At the subatomic level, we cannot observe anything without changing it. There is no such thing as an independent observer who can stand on the sideline watching the world race by without influencing it. The Von Neumann formula takes this finding even further by proclaiming that the action of the conscious observer alters that which is observed and the *intention* of the observer also affects the physical world. For better or worse, *each one of us affects everyone and everything around us.*

Whether through simple observation or by more complicated human intent, our connection to the energy around us is altered, thereby affecting the outcome of any circumstance. If my intention is positive or loving, the outcome will be more beneficial than if my intention is negative or hateful. What we send out into the world has a way of coming back to us. This is why it is so important to *live life with loving intention.*

Modern culture has looked to science to solve all of humankind's dilemmas, including our level of life satisfaction. But problems of a spiritual nature demand spiritual solutions that put to use spiritual tools, such as forgiveness, love, acceptance, humility, and surrender. While spiritual problems are not a result of a dysfunction in the brain, they can lead to unhealthy neurobiological changes. Dissatisfaction in life is a problem derived from a spiritual sense of a lack of wholeness created by the human ego.

Science improves and saves lives, but the spiritual domain is where healing and happiness reside. In this book, I present this truth to you from my own life experiences. While it's true that subjective experiences cannot be proven per se, there is a "knowingness" that comes from walking through the fire and coming out the other end that is of great, if not greater, value than scientific objectivity. The experience and knowingness gained from being a survivor—whether from addiction, depression, loss of a loved one, or other life-altering event—creates an opportunity for each of us to evolve to a higher spiritual plane. *When seized, life's tragedies become spiritual opportunities.*

The ego is our "false self," "mind," or "small self." It knows of no power greater than itself. It is self-serving and is constantly battling for survival or personal gain. It is always fighting against or fleeing from some perceived fear. It will do whatever it takes to relieve itself of life's "miseries." But it always fails. Its self-destructive line of thinking can drive us into maladaptive behaviors designed to serve only the ego. To the ego, no one else matters. *The ego is the source of all human misery.*

In order for correction to take place—in other words, for joy to replace misery—there must be a change in character. There must be a simple but profound return to the Self—our Divine nature or soul. Reclaiming the Self brings spiritual healing and transformation.

This is a book about healing. It is not about symptom reduction. I will show you how the ego develops and how it causes all of the suffering in our lives. I will also endeavor to show you who you really are: the Self. The Self is God immanent and is the source of happiness and unconditional love. This book is about a journey of discovery. It is about a return to the Self.

At the end of all our exploring, we will arrive where we started and know the place for the first time!
—T.S. ELIOT

The Creation of the World: A Hindu Parable

"Now that we have the earth and the sky and the mountains and the rivers and the moon and the stars, we will create man. Where shall we hide the truth of his being from him?" asked God.

One angel said, "Let's hide it on the highest mountaintop."

And to this God responded, "No, eventually he will learn to scale the mountains. He will find it."

"Let's take it down to the very deepest part of the ocean," another angel suggested.

"No, eventually, man will learn how to go to the darkest, deepest part of the ocean. Do not hide it there," said God.

"Well, let's hide it on the moon, then," said yet another angel.

"No, eventually he'll reach the moon as well," God replied.

They continued this way for a time before the answer came to them all at once. They knew exactly where to hide the truth where humankind would never look for it: within himself.

This is a very old Hindu parable from the oral tradition that has no discernable original source. In all spiritual traditions, the common theme is that as humans, we are always on a quest to find God and our true Self. To do this, we have a tendency to always look outside of ourselves for the truth, but all of the great teachers, saints, and sages have said that there is a place inside of each of us that is absolutely holy, pure, and divine: it is God, and the kingdom of God is within us. We are spiritual beings and Divine by nature. We are not God, but God is within us.

Traditional Western thought often ignores the vast insights provided by the Eastern methods of spiritual transformation. Many Westerners are groomed to measure their worthiness by how much power, control, and security they've achieved. The deep mystery of life has been replaced by a superficial ego game based on the acquisition of material gain, how to have better sex, winning others' approval, and so on. This pursuit has caused anxiety and deadened our sensitivity to the dignity of the Self—our Divine nature. The infinite spiritual domain has been replaced by alienating terminologies, and instead of viewing wounds to our egos as opportunities for spiritual growth, we litigate. While there is a great scarcity of legitimate transformational spiritual wisdom in our society, there is a lot of song and dance about how to become self-actualized (to "fully realize one's potential").

All of this has left many of us in a state of spiritual crisis. When in crisis, we generally seek the help of psychiatrists, psychologists, social workers, therapists, and other clinicians. Although well-meaning, intelligent, and knowledgeable, our mental-health educational system fails to teach a proper understanding of the spiritual world and its role in healing. While mental-health experts can help reduce symptoms, this is not enough. Most of our deepest problems are spiritual in nature. Psychotherapy and mood-altering prescription drugs have little effect on these difficulties of living.

Healing in its true sense goes way beyond the superficial

nature of symptom relief. Healing means the removal of the cause of our suffering, which resides in the ego. Every spiritual journey is a movement away from the ego to that which we really are—the Self. The Self is God immanent (the Divine within us). It is the breath of life given to each of us as a gift of love, joy, and happiness. We are born with this gift, for it is who we truly are. However, as we grow and begin to experience the world, we lose track of this gift. Attaching to things outside of ourselves, we place our energy into objects, believing those things will make us happy. This kind of happiness is superficial and fleeting. It never works. It's like the first scratch on a brand-new car—inevitable and devastating. Healing, or true contentment, comes when we realize that we brought absolutely nothing into this world and can take nothing out of it.

In order to grow spiritually, we must come out of the shadows of our egoic, narcissistic self-centeredness. We cannot expect people and things to give us the peace and love we desire, although we endow them with this ability. Only in a return to our core can we begin to find our Self. It is the spiritual journey—not any particular destination—that holds the clues to our yearning for peace, joy, and love.

All human life unfolds within an infinite energy field of consciousness. Each life is beset by challenges that are, in fact, opportunities for spiritual growth. These spiritual opportunities can lead us from humiliation to humility and the experience of humanity. In other words, humility leads to a humble acknowledgment of what it means to be human. The field of consciousness is comprised of the power of transforming energy. It is available to you and me. If we tap into this energy, we join our place in the great mystery of creation. Hidden within us is a replica of the mystery, but many of us are simply not aware of this power or presence. Because we are unconscious of this awesome mystery, it is not reflected in our lives, our characters, or, especially, our hearts. We do not recognize the transforming power that can shine forth when honestly beckoned. However, I believe that we all share a basic call to transcend the selfishness and suffering of our egos and come into contact with the Divine within. When you recognize it, you will know that you are home.

Primal Fears

Alienation and death are our most primal fears. Take comfort in knowing that you are part of the field of consciousness and can therefore never be alone, and because the Self, our Divine nature or Soul, lives forever, we never die. Once we move beyond these fears, we can begin to ease the unconscious fears that continue to cause us suffering. Fears about our worthiness and fears about our need for power and control, for example, cause us to place our happiness in the hands of people and circumstances rather than where it belongs— through an abiding faith in God.

Who Am I?

I am not a theologian. Other than Adam, it is impossible for one to say that all of his/her words are truly original. Along the way, I have encountered many good teachers and have been, I believe, a good student. Unfortunately, I could not always tell whether the lessons were positive or negative ones. I have tried to give credit throughout this text to those whose teachings were positive, valuable, and timely.

My path to get here seemed like the "pinball theory of life." Much like many of your life paths, I suppose, it was tortuous and, at times, very twisted. My high school biology teacher taught me that nerves operate on the principle of "all or nothing." This is the way I thought of my early life. In college we called ourselves "maxers" and prided ourselves on taking everything—especially alcohol and drugs—to the extreme. There was never enough alcohol or drugs, and no amount could fill up the hole within us. We were thirsting for something that the alcohol and drugs could not give us. *Where do you go when you have gone too far?* The way back home—back to the Self—is an existentially lonely one, and I took many wrong directions.

The sixteen-century mystic Saint John of the Cross said, "Silence is God's first language." Life is different now, thanks to God and compassionate people who have changed my life. Silence and solitude have replaced screaming guitars. The constant "chatter" of the left hemisphere of my brain has been replaced by the silence and serenity of the right hemisphere. The spiritual journey has pulled me from the future into a spiritual state best described as "enlighten-ment." This was not something I could do on my own, but was a gift from God.

I am very grateful and humbled to be a follower of Jesus Christ and to try in my inept, human way to live up to his ideals, sharing what I have learned along the way. I believe that if the spiritual approach is not in everything we do and are a part of—schools, government, families—then nothing will ever work out right. It is only in the spiritual, nonlinear world that everything just seems to work out.

Mine is a story of movement and grace and of losing in order to ultimately win. The movement is a steep climb up a mountain from which I can see reality from an expanded perspective.

I do not know anything, but I have knowingness about the spiritual realm and the paths I took on my journey to the state of enlightenment. I cannot prove anything to you. Regardless of what you think of me and my experiences, please judge the messages in this book on their own merit. This book is my attempt to explain the knowingness that God has granted to me. I have no interest in converting any-one or trying to change others. Attempts to do so do not work. In the Buddhist sense, I ask that you keep an open mind and use the world as your wet lab. If the message fits, use it. Otherwise, discard it.

How can we accept that the world is perfect just the way God created it and that all suffering is caused by the ego? How can we trust in God and have the faith that He will care for us if we ask? Why does bad stuff happen? Know that these challenges are opportunities to increase your level of spiritual consciousness and get closer to God. Everything simply depends on the way it is observed and understood. For example, hitting bottom due to alcoholism or another addiction is a wake-up call that tells us we have gone too far and that it is time to return home. An alcoholic or addict is not truly who we are. We are God immanent, the Self. The ego has submerged the Self behind an endless morass of definitions, both good and bad, that affect our mood states. But always remember, there really is only one true, joyous you: the Self you were born with. Happiness is our birthright as a result of the Divine nature found in all of us.

When our biological needs for *security and survival, affection and esteem*, and *power and control* are developmentally repressed or compensated for by unhealthy means, the ego turns outside of itself to find happiness. Fr. Thomas Keating, a leader in contemplative prayer, refers to these categories as "egoic value systems for happiness." We will be looking at these in depth in Chapter 2. Misplaced desires become avenues for failed experimentation. It is in spiritual recovery that we find true healing. The use of spiritual tools—forgiveness, surrender, humility, unconditional love, gratitude, acceptance, and so on—are necessary to alleviate the spiritual maladies of desire, pride, fear, helplessness, and guilt.

Throughout this book I will attempt to help you on your

spiritual journey toward a return to your Self, and I will share my personal story of grace on my own journey home. In Chapters 1, 2, and 3, I describe the development of the fear-based human ego and how its distorted beliefs—including the belief that happiness can be found outside of ourselves—cause all the suffering in the world. In Chapters 4 through 10, I discuss the spiritual journey of transformation, which leads to the disassembly of the ego and describe various spiritual paths, techniques, and tools that will help you get there. I hope you will find something of yourself in this journey. It is my utmost wish that this book will inspire you in your own spiritual voyage. Thank you for giving me the opportunity to enter your world.

As the Buddha taught, "Rare is it to be born a human being, rarer still to have heard of Enlightenment, and even rarer still to pursue it."

1

How It Is: No More "Me"

"Enter in through the narrow door, for wide is the door and broad is the road which leads to destruction, and many are those who travel on it. O how narrow is the door and how difficult is the road which leads to life and few are those who are found on it."[1]

—Jesus speaking in the Gospel of Matthew 7:13–14

---

[1] Matthew 7:13–14, *Holy Bible from the Ancient Eastern Text*, trans. George M. Lamsa (San Francisco: HarperCollins, 1933).

Our first leg on the spiritual journey involves ridding ourselves of our egos. Jesus said, "For he who wishes to save his life
shall lose it; but he who loses his life for my sake shall save it"
(Luke 9:24). While this saying seems like a paradox, to experience spiritual transformation, we must surrender everything
to God—every opinion, every motive, every action, every prejudice—in fact, our entire lives. Both trust and love are necessary to transcend the ego—trust in the existence of a higher
reality, which I personally call God, and love for this higher
reality, as well as an intense longing to realize it. Surrendering
everything to God—all that we are attached to through the ego,
including our very lives—is a path to ultimate freedom.

Once we get beyond all egoic attachments to life, there is a
raw base energy that is Divine. It is unconditional love, a warm-
hearted, cohesive, purposeful intelligence. This is *le point vierge*
(virgin point). It is the center not touched by sin and illusion; a
point of pure truth; a spark belonging only to God. It is the
secret center of the heart that only God penetrates. In order to
reach this point, we must completely empty ourselves and, in
our poverty, be receptive to His will and His will only.

When we have the courage and determination to surrender
all to God, the "I," "me," and "mine" of the ego are gone. They
are replaced by a persona that lives in this earthly world but is
not attached to it. We live for the next world, whatever that
might be. The false self of the ego is absorbed into the Self,
who sees the essence of things and is not distracted by the

egoic notions of comparison and contrast, ownership and personal gain. What remains exists for service to others and sees the world as perfectly just the way God planned it. There is little need for material things, and Madison Avenue marketing doesn't work, because the greed and grandiosity of the ego that fueled it no longer exist. This loss of the ego also rids one of the fear of death, for death is an illusion: only the illusory self can die, since the Self is eternal.

After surrendering everything to God, I experienced incredible anger and rage as my ego sought to stave off its ultimate fate. The ego is very manipulative and is all about survival. There were several people who, because of their lack of integrity, had caused my ego much anger and frustration. The ego raged at these individuals as it fought for its survival as a separate entity. The intensity of the anger was quite shocking to me, as it was far beyond anything I could remember experiencing before. Then, at some point, my body became overwhelmed by severe abdominal pain. After each bout of pain, cramping, and vomiting, the attempt to surrender this agony to God was met with more of the same.

Somewhere in my mind—after a long period of struggling to surrender—I recalled Elisabeth Kübler-Ross's story of enlightenment. In her story, she described an acceptance of her pain. I received the awareness that the ego was not an enemy and could not be surrendered or dispensed with, but must be assimilated into the Self. The ego must be loved into wholeness and thus transformed but not rejected. Love and acceptance of the pain led to instantaneous relief, remarkably with no residual effect, after hours of vomiting and heaving. All was replaced with a sense of calm, and I could finally catch my breath. In this awakened state, I discovered that reality is in essence the glory of the Divine and our true nature is love.

The next twelve hours of my life are difficult to explain. There was no sense of time or place. In the subjective, nonlinear world, there is no time. Christian writers call the experience "mystical union" and the Vedantists call it "Samadhi" (a superconscious state; the fourth type of consciousness after waking, dreaming, and dreamless sleep). The Bengali mystic Sri Ramakrishna linked the occurrence of Samadhi to the rising of kundalini energy or the "spiritual current." I had been preparing for this experience for a long time, but it was like nothing I could have imagined. My mind was totally overwhelmed by an incredibly powerful energy or infinitely great force that rendered it completely silent. The only event in my life that was even remotely similar was when, as a child, I stood a few feet away from a railroad track and felt the immense power as a train roared by.

The room and everything in it were no longer visible, and the very source of consciousness itself was revealed. All of the beauty of Divinity shone forth, revealing that every breath we take and everything we see, smell, or touch is the language of God. God's radiance was totally consuming and overpowering, yet delightful. Although this experience was incredibly powerful and overwhelming, it was as gentle as a small child. I sensed a connectedness to everything. To say it was stunning is a gross understatement. Everything shimmered, and every movement seemed involuntary and slow. The field of consciousness, what I believe to be the Holy Spirit, was a brilliant white not of this earth. At its core was a mother-of-pearl-like cauldron of energy, and at the periphery was a vibrating, quivering energy without a beginning or end. At first, I was capable of observing this energy field. Later, I would become one with the field, as there was an awareness of nonconceptuality—that is, no difference between subject and object.

At some point, a sense of fear pervaded me as I suddenly had an awareness of evil emanating from the small room next to the one I was in. Then, to my mind came the assertion that "fear is an illusion; walk through it." When I looked directly into the room, I could see an indistinct energy force from my peripheral vision and sensed from it the absence of love. From my "knowingness" came the thought, *Where is the love . . . where is the love of God? I want no part of anything that is absent of God no matter how powerful it might appear.* I am unsure of how I managed to acquire a Bible—perhaps it was an out-of-body experience; perhaps it happened only in my neural structure; perhaps I retrieved it from somewhere—but Psalms 23 and 91 came to me for protection, especially these words from Psalm 91:

Because he has loved me,

Therefore will I deliver him;

I will set him on high because he has known my name.

He shall call upon me, and I will answer him;

I will be with him in trouble;

I will deliver him and honor him.[2]

This was the abyss of the void I'd come across so often in my readings—the ultimate duality of "allness" versus nothingness, the ultimate pair of opposites to transcend. The void is infinite but devoid of context. It is absent of God's love. Many have been stuck there. I have read that the void is the last trick up the ego's sleeve. This is a trap even well-known spiritual seekers have fallen into. But the void is an illusion. There is no opposite to the love of God. Allness versus nothingness is a classical duality that, in this instance, needed to be refused—and I did.

Until this point, I had a sense of being able to differentiate myself from the totality of the immense eternal field of vibrating energy. Now the experience intensified, and I was no longer differentiated from the field at all. I was the field, and the field was me. There really was no more *I* or *me*. The suffusion of light and the presence of infinite love with no beginning and no end was undifferentiated from the Self. This was the point where all forms converged into oneness. In the

---

[2] Psalm 91:14–15, *Holy Bible,* trans. George M. Lamsa.

Gospels, Jesus frequently refers to this point as "the light." Nonlinear consciousness certainly involves the ability "to make the two become one."

The Gospel of Thomas consists of 114 short sayings or logia (Greek for "sayings" or "aphorisms"). Logion 22 states:

> When you are able
> To make two become one,
> The inside like the outside,
> And the outside like the inside,
> And the above like the below,
> And when you make the male and the female
>   one and the same,
> So that the male not be male nor the female female;
> And when you fashion eyes in the place of an eye,
> And a hand in place of a hand,
> And a foot in place of a foot,
> And a likeness in place of a likeness;
> Then will you enter the kingdom.[3]

I have no firsthand recollection of how long this experience lasted, perhaps twelve hours or so. Later on, I was able to piece it together from reports from my family. In the following days, it took an effort to become used to the silence of my mind. There was no chatter, nothing telling me to go do this or go do that. It

---

[3] http://www.gnosis.org/naghamm/gthlamb.html.

was a bit disconcerting. Sometimes, I'd have a sense of loneliness without my mind's chatter. Today, this is a wonderful grace. To be able to be in the silence of consciousness without interruption is a gift of tranquility. It is the peace beyond all understanding.

Everything shone forth radiantly, and I spent a lot of time outdoors. My yard blessedly sits beside the Wekiva Preserve, where families of deer, wild turkeys, peacocks, and rabbits, as well as a lone bobcat or panther, often present themselves at various times. Every animal, plant, and tree shone forth in true, vivid splendor, and the vast beauty and perfection of creation was sometimes overwhelming.

From this point on, I had a connectedness to all things. Without the judgmentalism of the ego, one sees things as they truly are—splendid, beautiful, fully alive, and connected to everything else in the universe. Without the ego's tendency to live in the past and future, one is ever present in the moment. The moment is peaceful, connected to everything and without guilt or fear. Sometimes I am amazed at how close things feel. It is as if in certain moments there is no separation between myself and trees or the deer that come into the yard. Everything is astoundingly universal and connected.

A Search for "Something"

From a very early age, I felt there was something greater to be learned and experienced in this life. As it happened, the search for this "something" led me in a number of directions. Around the age of fourteen, my thoughts were leaning toward Christian ministry. By age sixteen, these thoughts were replaced by what seemed to be an easier and better answer: alcohol and drugs. It wasn't that I was necessarily going in the wrong direction; I was just using the wrong means to get there.

Many of us want to transcend that which we perceive ourselves to be. Some try sex or drugs, while others turn to food, gambling, shopping, and so on. For me, the path I chose to achieve higher consciousness was to alter my brain with chemicals. While some of the drugs brought me close to what I was seeking, I could never hold on to that feeling of connection. This is because it was a connection built on ego.

Desire for "something more" comes from a sense of lack and incessantly drives us to try to fill the hole that exists within us. This is described by Aldous Huxley in his classic *The Doors of Perception*, where he states, "It has always seemed to me possible that, through hypnosis, for example, or autohypnosis, by means of systematic meditation, or else by taking the appropriate drug, I might so change my ordinary mode of consciousness as to be able to know, from the inside, what the visionary, the medium, even the mystic were talking about."[4]

The problem with the drug experience—like other external approaches to happiness—is that one cannot own it; it is always fleeting. You can get so close—only to have it slip away.

---

[4] Aldous Huxley, *The Doors of Perception*, accessed online at http://www.mescaline.com/huxley.htm.

Looking out at the field behind my house and watching the trees rustle, I can go back to 1969 when I used cocaine for the first time at a farmhouse outside of Fredericksburg, Virginia. I recall saying to God, "Where has this been all of my life? This is the way I always wanted to feel!" This is the chase, and it is endless, because we can never really own and possess that sense of peace and connection that comes from drug use. For example, instead of helping me find my Self, drugs just caused me to get lost in my bathroom. And so it goes, on and on, as if there will never be an end to the search.

Let me give you my definition of the Self. It starts with the understanding that the kingdom of God is within all of us. This is stated in the Bible and many holy texts, as well as by wise and holy teachings from many spiritual traditions. The Self is the life energy (also called the Soul) breathed into Adam and is the basis of who we really are—children of God. It has always been and will always be. It is on a journey. The Self comes from the Light, and its journey is back to the Light. We are all perfect; perfectly on that journey back home to where we all started. Along the way there are trials and tribulations, which I call spiritual opportunities, circumstances that allow us to move along that path back home.

When I was a small child, my friends and I were happiness waiting to happen. We played hide-and-seek, kick the can, and tag. As it is for small children, our joy was an internally generated phenomenon. But somewhere along the way, I became lost to the experience of this type of joy, as did my friends. We got older, and we attributed any happiness we felt to the use of alcohol and drugs. Without the drugs, there was neither joy nor wonder. As the old saying from the 1960s goes, "There's just no hope without a little more dope." We were searching for something we didn't quite understand at the time, but we were searching nonetheless—always searching for something we already possessed.

We didn't have a clue about how our brains worked. Alcohol and drugs alter experience by causing changes in neural operations (scientists call this *toxicity*, while addicts call it a darn good "buzz"). Neurotransmitters and receptors in various areas of the brain are altered secondary to drinking alcohol and taking other mood-altering substances. If these neurotransmitters and receptors were not available, the substance would end up in the toilet without appreciable effect. If asked, "What makes you high—the drug or your brain?" we would have answered incorrectly. No sensation can be caused by an external substance that the brain cannot achieve on its own.

By giving any inanimate object control over our lives, we allow it to dominate us. My friends and I no longer controlled the happiness in life—rather, life controlled us. We were just trying to find ourselves. All of us were trying to discover our Self. It never dawned on us that we couldn't find what we already had—at least not outside of ourselves. No amount of money, college degrees, fine cars, or beautiful homes lived up to their promise of happiness. We were left wondering, *What's the next great thing "to get," or "to have," or "to try"?* Our search for gaining happiness outside of ourselves left us in despair.

Despair is suffering that fails to teach. We had to learn that it is the attitude of sacrifice and acceptance that turns suffering into joy. By suffering, I do not mean needless egoic suffering, but faithfully enduring the consequences of the human condition without being manipulated by the ego. It is true that we grow by dying to the false self and rising again to higher levels of awareness through spiritual growth and transformation.

The contemplative Thomas Merton said it well: "I cannot discover God in myself and myself in Him unless I have the courage to face myself exactly as I am, with all my limitations, and to accept others as they are, with all their limitations."[5]

A man asked his spiritual teacher, "How can I be more like you?" The teacher replied, "To be more like me you need to be more like you." It also helps to have the courage to not give up before the miracle happens.

The Ego-Driven State

What is it about our brains that make them so personally and intersubjectively secretive and misguided? The answer to this and all forms of human suffering is the ego. The ego wants to look at every mystery from its own perspective. *How in the world could God allow me to go through so much suffering and*

---

[5] Thomas Merton, *No Man Is an Island* (San Diego: Harcourt, 1955), xvi.

pain? All challenges are potential spiritual opportunities. However, it is all quite mysterious and unknowable. Quantum physics studies the subatomic world and notices it does not follow the rules expected of nature (laws of classical or Newtonian physics). It is beyond our current understanding, at least from the scientific paradigm. All we can say is, "I don't understand." In our limited world where we see so little and hear a very narrow range of sound, we expect God to act like we would act in our ego-driven state. It is our own thinking— the delusions, judgments, and obsessions espoused by the ego—that must be questioned. It is our limited view, our imprecise perspective, that is questionable. God is doing just fine without any help from us.

Nothing real can be threatened, and nothing unreal exists. Planted in each of us is the knowingness of the eternal Self. The mind cannot grasp this—it is knowingness without need of explanation or requiring any form of defense. It just is. Many of us refer to our bodies as "I." We are not our bodies. In physical reality, science tells us that the body is made up of "stuff" called atoms with neutrons, electrons, nuclei, and so on. We are each actually 99.9 percent space. The important question becomes, what is the 0.1 percent physical reality? This 0.1 percent isn't really stuff at all but vibrating energy or light. We come from the Light (or the breath of life) and are on a journey back to the source of that Light. So, in essence, as vibrating light, we are all just little light shows residing in an infinite light show called consciousness.

How My Search for Truth Began

Desire and the pride of the ego stand in the way of real spiritual progress. Pride does not allow us to view our own character defects and locks us into a negative spiral of always blaming everyone and everything else for life's troubles. The secondary gain of the ego allows the ego to benefit even when it looks like it is suffering. Situations in life that cause negative emotions such as anger are actually positive to the ego. It can always blame someone or something else. The resulting resentment gives the ego carte blanche in regard to behavior as it is always someone or something causing me to be angry, to fail, not to get my way, to drink, or to overeat. The ego doesn't take responsibility, so it is trapped in a never-ending cycle of self-delusion and self-defeat. This blame cast on others leads to resentments. These resentments keep us spiraling downward, providing an excuse for participating in self-defeating behavior. *Somebody else made me do it. If they only had given me my way, this would not have happened to me.* In all cases of exaggerated pride, humility is the ultimate force of interruption. Depending on one's perspective, humiliation is the crash landing that generally forces us, through sheer pain of existence, to look more closely at our hurt, loneliness, and pain.

For me, it was the hopeless state of addiction compounded by marijuana misdemeanors, going to prison, and the ultimate letter from the dean of the School of Pharmacy at the Medical College of Virginia that started to get my attention. In a short and curt letter of dismissal, the dean stated, "May God help you find another way in life." He was clairvoyant, although I didn't realize it at the time.

Behind all of my self-defeating behaviors was an occurrence that precipitated my life's tailspin. At age eighteen, my father died of what was diagnosed as liver and kidney failure. Actually, it was alcohol related. In my mind, my father was one of the greatest men who had ever lived. In truth, he had many fine features as well as self-defeating flaws. He was human.

In the little town in Virginia where we lived, my father was a hero. He was a cardiologist who saved people's lives. He was compassionate and truly loved medicine and helping people. His character was gentle, and I used to love to go to the hospital with him to hear him talk to patients. They were not just a number; he truly cared for them, and his bedside manner was genuine and compassionate.

My father, Camden, for whom I was named, was not only an alcoholic but a workaholic. He had time for his patients but not for his two children. I know he loved us, but he was unable to truly show his emotions. On several occasions, he'd press money into my palm as I left the house to go back to school. It was his way of telling me he cared for me, but money wasn't what I really needed from him. I went in search of affection and self-esteem, hoping somehow the alcohol, drugs, or other people in my life would somehow let me know I was all right. Unfortunately, the other people in my life were looking for the same things I was looking for. I was in the company of misery and broken dreams.

My father was taken from his office by ambulance to intensive care where he died several days later. I remember standing by his bed, wanting to say some things to him and hoping he would tell me he loved me, but neither one of us could rise to that terminal moment. I replayed the scene for years, always hoping it would turn out differently. His death caused me incredible pain, and I made a decision to repress love because it hurt too much. With vivid memory, I recall sitting in my bedroom when one of the town's business leaders presented me with my father's bronze shingle from his office door. It read Cardwell C. Nuckols, Sr., M.D. The gentleman said, "Keep this nameplate, and when you graduate from medical school, the town will get you an office that you can put this bronze plaque on." There was no doubt in my mind that I could never be as good as he was.

My earlier love of God was also repressed, and I became concerned with living life alone, independent, without needing anything from anyone. I commenced a six-year slide into the depths of addiction hell, later switching addictions to workaholism. During those years, my God became science, and it was my hope that science would explain all of the mysteries of this world. The German philosopher and critic Friedrich Nietzsche said, "God is dead." What he meant was that science would discover all of the universal mysteries, and there would be no need for God, as man would control his universe. How wrong he was. How wrong I was. Twenty-five years ago, I realized this was not going to happen—not only not in my life but probably never. Out of sheer fear and longing for something better than the aloneness of existence, my search for truth began.

These instances in life are often looked upon as overwhelming times devoid of personal control. Faced with one, I pondered the existence of a benevolent God. How could a loving God allow such misery and pain to enter one's life? If such a God existed, did I really want to be a believer in such an entity? This sort of painful dissonance overwhelms the ego. It is at moments like this that a spiritual opportunity is presented. Looking back on that time in my life and others subsequent to and later in life, the pain, emptiness, and existential loneliness created a crack in my ego, allowing the Holy Spirit to begin its work. Although it took years for me to realize it, this was a spiritual opportunity.

The tragedy of human life interests me—those points when the ego is shattered, thereby allowing the Holy Spirit to shine and do Its work. These tragedies are opportunities to get closer to God. The Holy Spirit is a power, not a person. It is the spirit of God, a Divine gift. It is a source of joy to the heart and light to the eyes, and creates life on a whole new level of spiritual awareness. It cultivates and inspires kindness, goodness, gentleness, and charity. The Holy Spirit is a gift of spiritual wisdom to be used for the betterment of humankind. As you will learn throughout this book, the incredible power of the Holy Spirit transformed my being.

Today I thank God for my misfortunes. It is true that humiliation goes before humility. What seemed so unfair and unfortunate at the time turned out to be a turning point leading to spiritual transformation. The world may not have changed, but spiritual growth has allowed me to see the world from a very different perspective. The world does look quite different when we accept our condition and stop trying to control people, places, and things. When the ego is deflated and humility manifests, defiance and grandiosity fade. We can now accept life on life's own terms.

As composer and jazz musician John McAndrew sings in "Give Me New Eyes":

When black clouds come over me,
They darken my skies
If it's how I look at things
Then give me new eyes ... give me new eyes.[6]

Always the most real and important work is that which is accomplished deep within one's soul, leading to an increased capacity for love and service to others. It is imperative to note that love is not an emotion but is actually a way of being in the

---

[5] Used by permission of M. Andrew Music.

world. There is no opposite of love as it is unconditional in its quality. Unconditional love cannot be purchased at any price. It can only be freely given from the heart. It is love and humility that deflates the ego and allows for true joy in living. It is only through selfless service to others that we find true personal happiness. This is the Divine paradox of "giving it away to keep it."

The Spiritual Journey

The great spiritual traditions of both East and West, although different in their methods, agree that by spiritual discipline a person can radically change his/her life and attain deeper meaning and more complete integration. We can radically change and find more complete fulfillment and greater freedom of spirit than can ever be found in the pursuit of material goods and money. There is more to human life than just trying to "get somewhere." All spiritual traditions believe that the highest ambition lies well beyond worldly ambition and the narcissistic requirements of the ego. These traditions tell us that spirit can achieve higher and higher degrees of illumination, leading to a greater understanding of the meaning and purpose of life.

God wants us to become intimate with Him and, in the process, fulfill our spiritual destinies. Along the way, we learn many hard lessons. Every one of us is on a journey—a journey back home. This is the essence of human desire. We all want to be connected and loved deep down inside. However, attachment to worldly things takes the energy of the life force and channels it away from the true source of our desire: intimacy with God.

Attachment to people, places, and things of this world lead us into sorrow and addiction. We often place more value in obtaining things than in attaining the true source of our desire. Then we must protect what we have obtained. This "owning" is a proxy for our true desire—the realization of our connectedness with God. Whenever we value worldly things more than the love of God, we set ourselves up for attachment and addiction. Somehow, in one of these lifetimes, we need to learn how to detach from these worldly compulsions and obsessions, thus allowing for a pure union with the Divine (enlightenment).

We are all perfect. We are just perfectly where we need to be in order to take advantage of the opportunities for spiritual growth in this lifetime. God knows there are many such opportunities. Being human gives us the opportunity to make spiritual decisions every moment. In these decisions, the lessons of life are learned. The lessons of life can be hard, but each one gives us an opportunity to move beyond where we are spiritually to a higher knowledge of ourselves, our world, and our relationship with God.

I have learned over the years that all true spiritual paths lead to the same ultimate outcome, but only with discipline and "one-sightedness" of effort. All true spiritual paths can lead to enlightenment—that intimate relatedness to God, the return to the Light, or deeper self-knowledge. Similarly, even those events in life that seem the least "spiritual" or "connected" in nature—the challenges, obstacles, and hardships of every life—can become spiritual events of great value when there is a desire for spiritual growth.

This is a journey of many opportunities. By this I mean it involves many different embodiments over the course of history. There is only one life, however. That is the life of the Self or soul. It doesn't die, as it is eternal, struggling toward home as it moves back toward its Creator.

You can spend your time living in the past, wondering why things happened to you the way they did and how unfair all of this was. You can spend your life in the future, dreaming about how things will be if everything goes right. However, there is a third option: surrender to the present moment and understand that everything is just as God planned so that you can learn the lessons you were sent here to learn. I recommend the third option. Anything other than living in the moment is akin to death.

In my own personal experience, the urge to reach the state of enlightenment was intense. If I was going to go for something greater, I wanted to go as far and as fast as God would allow me to. I generally spent four to six hours every day in prayer and meditation or studying spiritual writings. The techniques of the contemplative Christian movement of the first few hundred years after Christ yielded valuable information, as did the work of other contemplatives such as Saint John of the Cross and Thomas Merton. The original words of Jesus in the New Testament, and especially the Beatitudes, entered the picture. (The Beatitudes, found in Matthew 5:3–12, are the nonlinear path Jesus left with us to lead us to enlightenment.) It seemed like one thing led me to another and then to another, all along revealing a path. Very quickly, I started to be pulled from the future. There was no real effort of my own. Everything happened on its own, as I was engaged with the Divine. My life literally became a prayer, and there was nothing else to think about. I saw divinity in everything and beauty everywhere, even in those whose lives were out of control at the time.

There are many paths to God, but I had to start somewhere. I made a decision to follow a path of action and the heart. (These paths and others will be discussed in depth later.) This decision began with an absolute agreement to be kind to everyone and everything and especially myself all of the time without exception for a period of eight weeks. At the end of the eight weeks, I was incapable of being mean or unkind. For example, at the end of the seventh week, I missed the last flight out of Cincinnati at eleven at night. Knowing I would not be able to be where I was supposed to teach the next morning, I said something to the gate agent that was not very nice. It felt like a knife was thrust into my side, and I proceeded to apologize profusely. (I was probably more obnoxious in my apology than in my brief display of negative emotion.) The fact was, however, my brain had changed, and a compassionate neural network had become well developed. Of course, when you are kind, you tend to be more forgiving, loving, and so on.

Soon thereafter I decided to forgive everyone, including myself, all of the time and to be humble, and to put others ahead of myself. With daily, intense, four to six hours of spiritual study, the path of negation of the mind or nonduality was initiated. All of the ego's motives, opinions, positionalities (character defects), and fear-based, unconscious programs for happiness were identified and turned over or surrendered to God.

As this part of the journey progressed, I was able to experience genuine happiness. I had never considered myself a happy person; perhaps my introversion and the tendency to see everything through critical lenses contributed to this. To be joyfully happy and to be able to see love and beauty in everything was almost beyond my comprehension. I always thought happiness was the ultimate, eternal goal. To be happy seemed like such a prize to someone who had only known it fleetingly.

The problem with happiness is that it needs contrast to highlight its goodness. There seems to be a necessary flatness or sadness needed to serve as a comparison. *I was sad, but now I am happy*, for example. If I am happy all of the time, it would stop feeling like happiness after a while.

I have discovered something greater than the brittle state of happiness: a peace beyond all understanding. It is like being buoyant in water and feeling the waves as they perpetually roll by. One of my great childhood memories is lying on a small float, feeling the sun on my body while the small waves lulled me into a different space. Later, I learned that this was the serenity and quiet of the right hemisphere of my brain. (I'll talk more about the left and the right hemispheres of the brain in Chapter 9.) There is no sense of before or after . . . just the rolling. Here there is no degree of time or space, just a steady state—an inner calm and smiles as the world goes by. This results from having detachment with love.

Pure consciousness is an abiding peace. From a place of detachment and peace beyond worldly understanding, the world is an entirely magnificent place. When one sees the essence of life and not the ego-gratifying sizzle of the American marketplace, life becomes funny and often absurd. You do not need further entertainment, as the human comedy is always going on around you.

Enlightenment is the end of the human journey of spiritual transformation, but it begins a new journey into the mystery. Sometimes, I wonder if it will be like waiting in line at Disney World. After proceeding along a convoluted line in one room, will I emerge at the end only to enter yet another room of long, convoluted lines? I tend to not think so, but it is a mystery after all.

Transformation is the natural unfolding of a human life. It is to become that which we truly are—the Self. Transformation is a return to our authentic Self after periods of the ego's willful desire to be in control of our lives. Transformation was the center point of early Christian beliefs. Transformation was Jesus's message to us. Not only did he teach it; he demonstrated it through His actions and left a path for us to follow. Following His path will take you to God.

Detachment

It has been nearly four years since the grace of the Holy Spirit transformed me. In reality, I do not exist anymore. What I mean is that there is no more separate self or ego that I once called "me." It has been replaced by utter silence. Yes, there is a persona called "I" in this book that acts and reacts to the world. But it is kind and gentle and sees the good in everyone and every situation, for everyone is right where they need to be on their personal journey back to the Light.

Over the years, my experience has "ripened." Not only has there been a rapid change in the level of spiritual consciousness but also a vertical deepening of understanding of what this state is all about. I am still a novice. There is not a sense of nonattachment from the world but of detachment. Detachment allows us to be free of the earthly desires that use up so much of our spiritual energy. These earthly desires are the basis of our addictions. We become attached to earthly things (from the French word *attaché* meaning "nailed to") and lose sight of our original, true desire for the love of God. Being detached allows all energy to be channeled toward God's will. The first two commandments reveal His will, telling us to "love your God with all your heart, and with all your soul, and with all your power, and with all your mind" and to "love your neighbor as you love yourself" (Matt. 22:37–39).

In the eyes of the world, I am less functional now. There is no anger when others think there should be. There is also no fear. Throughout our lives we have been conditioned to believe that efficiency is more admirable and productive than love. I now put love before efficiency. The old voice used to say, "You should be in control." The new voice is pure silence, which, as Saint John of the Cross said, is the first language of God.

Each day I pray for the pureness of faith without doubt. There is no way to determine what the future holds. Until further notice from God, I will continue to teach and be as helpful as I can be to others. Sometimes I don't feel in any way connected to this world. Other times, I seem to know exactly why I am here. Everything seems beautifully seamless and continuous.

The Self is a wellspring of hope. Hope is an abiding state of being. What if mystical hope is the intended state leading toward Divine fulfillment? I am talking about a hope not based on outcome but coming from the reservoir of the heart; a bearable lightness of being and a peace beyond all understanding.

*   *   *

I share this story with you for many reasons. Most important, this is not just my story, but I believe your story too. If
you are reading this book, you clearly have an interest in personal, spiritual progression. You are on your own journey.
When you start to feel the pull from the future, and spiritual
reading, prayer, meditation, and/or contemplation becomes
easy and joyful, you are in the homestretch. This brings up the
second reason for writing this book. For me, the most difficult
part of the journey was finding a path that worked for me.
There are many paths to enlightenment. This book will
describe some paths and techniques for you to consider.

My hope is that you find something of yourself in this book
and that it helps you in your own search for that which already
exists inside of you—the presence of God. I sincerely hope you
discover the serenity, love, and happiness that is your
birthright. Look into an infant's eyes. See the joy and understand that is the journey back home. May God bless you, and
may your heart be open to His goodness.

Tao Te Ching
#48

In pursuit of knowledge,
every day something is added.
In the practice of the Tao,
every day something is dropped.
Less and less do you need to force things,
until finally you arrive at non-action.
When nothing is done,
nothing is left undone.
True mastery can be gained
by letting things go their own way.
It can't be gained by interfering.[7]

---

[7] http://academic.brooklyn.cuny.edu/core9/phalsall/texts/taote-v3.html#48.

2

The Formation of the Ego

Watch your thoughts, for they become words.

Watch your words, for they become actions.

Watch your actions, for they become habits.

Watch your habits, for they become character.

Watch your character, for it becomes your destiny.

—Author Unknown

Beneath the machinations of the mind is the true unconscious cause of our distress—a distress based in fear, causing
us to continually repeat difficulties experienced during our
youth on an unconscious level. It was Sigmund Freud who first
described this phenomenon. Freud felt the pervasive disease
of the human condition was a psychic remnant of inadequate
attention received during early life. This involved early-life
neglect or other forms of abuse, generally perceived throughout life as an "inner emptiness." He taught that for successful
change to take place, remembering the early forgotten aspects
of childhood was critical. Later in his career, however, he made
a dramatic shift to the present, claiming that these internalized difficulties of inadequate attention continued to repeat
themselves throughout one's life under certain circumstances.

Unconscious wounds from our early lives are repeated in
our interactions later in life, if the situation reproduces the
content of the early hurt. For example, if people are abused
early in life, when they are older, they may be attracted to
someone who will also abuse them. When they choose this
person, they do not *consciously* believe that this person is like
the person who violated their trust. However, the image of the
hurtful parent, for example, is like a beacon that guides them
to the familiar patterns of their earlier lives. It is the ego,
rather than the Self, who is attracted to this unhealthy pattern.
The one crucial and defining feature of this repetitive cycle is

that these people remain unaware as to why they repeatedly choose situations that repeat the earlier hurts.

For example, one of my former clients, Marcus, grew up in a home with an abusive, alcoholic father who often beat him when he came home drunk. At age twelve, Marcus decided he would never let anyone hurt him again. Later in life, he continually had problems with male authority figures. He got into a pushing match with a policeman and a fight with his boss. To make matters worse, as his alcoholism progressed, he became less able to control his rage. When asked about this lack of control, he replied, "It's like there is someone inside me who takes over, and I have no control."

During our sessions, Marcus had a hard time getting in touch with and expressing his emotions, and when asked about his rage, he would say, "I either don't feel anything or I feel too much." His repeated problems with male authority figures, including me, were beyond his conscious awareness and understanding. He could not see the connection until the history and pattern was bought to his attention. Marcus had always felt alone and lonely, and was looking for someone or something to make him feel secure. He searched for a job that would guarantee permanent employment. He searched for the perfect relationship in which he would not be hurt or abandoned. In other words, he searched for the impossible. Because of his neediness and fear of being alone, he was always alone. In its desperate need to protect itself no matter the cost, the ego became the source of all of Marcus's suffering. He was on a painful search for something that did not exist.

How does the ego develop and how does it create such misery? First of all, let's look at how the ego develops as we grow. There is no existence of the ego at birth, and its formation takes place primarily during ages two or three until about age ten. During these years, the brain is a marvelous receiver, but it has little or no capacity to analyze and distinguish between good and bad except on a very concrete level. The ego's foundation is formed by overidentifying with the programmed opinions, values, and beliefs stemming from the family, community, customs, and culture it is born into, as well as the defense mechanisms it creates to deal with emotional and physical pain.

When something hurts us so badly that we cannot consciously deal with it, we often suppress it, stuffing the suppressed energy into our unconscious being. Another way we deal with being hurt is by compensating for it by using alcohol, drugs, sex, food, shopping, and so on. When the suppressed energy starts to emerge and we feel overwhelmed, we eat, drink, use drugs, and so on. When we have to divert our energy from God and our own growth and relationships with important people in our lives, we end up in unhealthy relationships with inanimate objects (such as drugs, alcohol, food, etc.). This is called addiction. From this suppressed, painful affect, the ego develops its value systems for happiness.[8]

---

[8] Thomas Keating, *The Better Part* (New York: Continuum, 2002).

As mentioned in the introduction, Fr. Thomas Keating, one of the foremost teachers of contemplative prayer in the Christian tradition, lists three egoic value systems for happiness that create the source of all our misery: *security and survival, affection and esteem,* and *power and control.* These are the unconscious value systems, what I refer to as the ego's "unconscious programs for happiness," that guide our daily decisions and keep us from experiencing true happiness in life. They are based in fear over an unpredictable future. Because of this, they are an illusion. Whenever we give in to fear, it makes the fear more real, more solid. Every time we give in, our lives become smaller and more limited.

Every child needs to be affirmed and reassured. If the child does not receive this from caregivers, defensive strategies (ego defenses) and compensatory measures (looking outside of ourselves for satisfaction) often evolve. A child may get stuck at the developmental phase where the deprivation occurs. Over time, the defensive strategies the child uses to deal with this lack of care can harden into programs for happiness that are supported by his/her thoughts (motives, opinions, and so on), behaviors, and feelings. When the child becomes an adult, life experiences can trigger these unconscious early programs for happiness. Unfortunately, what was developed in an attempt to create happiness only creates repetitive suffering.

Take Marcus, for example, who said, "I will never feel this

way again." In his attempts to avoid pain, he caused more suffering. It is unfortunate that we cannot clearly see the relationship between early-life struggles and later-life sources of misery.

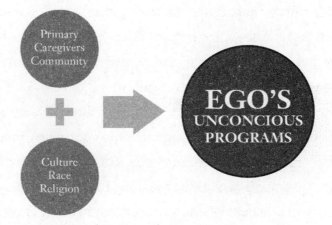

FIGURE 2.1. The ego is formed from a combination of primary caregiver messages and beliefs from the culture, nationality, religion, and race. This generally occurs between the ages of two and ten and is the source of much suffering, as these beliefs about self crystallize during adolescence and continue to harden until they become the ego's unconscious programs for happiness.

Security and Survival

The human brain is wired in such a way that the fear response is instinctually triggered by the first sign of real or perceived danger or insecurity. The danger does not have to be real; we only have to believe the danger is real for a cascade of neurochemical responses to be initiated. This automatic response is essentially the same response experienced by early

Homo sapiens when confronted by a saber-toothed tiger.

Now, think about a child growing up in an unpredictable, even dangerous environment, or in a family where the parents are often either physically or emotionally absent. For a child, being hurt or abandoned by their primary caregivers is a survival issue, since they are dependent upon these individuals, not just for food, shelter, and other basic survival needs, but also for love and acceptance.

Children who are raised in unsafe or unloving environments often "shut down" emotionally as a coping mechanism in order to escape their painful reality. They learn early on that showing any vulnerability to an abusing parent is often an invitation for additional abuse, so they learn coping skills, such as stuffing their emotions of fear, uncertainty, and unworthiness. Children who are raised without love and nurturing, and who, in fact, have often been abused physically and emotionally (and sometimes sexually), often carry their childhood coping skills into adulthood with them. Because of early-life development issues, such as fear of abandonment, feeling unworthy of love, and so on, as adults they may live in constant fear of being betrayed by those who should love them. They may also have an exaggerated sense of being unworthy of love, since they didn't receive it in early childhood.

For such a person, the aspects of life that most find enjoyable—being in a loving, committed relationship, feeling comfortable with solitude—are not achievable because they are unable to reveal their vulnerability and low self-esteem. Now consider subsequent relationships with other significant people and caregivers (therapists, teachers, etc.). When these individuals believe the people they have relationships with are going to leave them, whether real or perceived, they become very anxious and impulsive. Their behavior may, in fact, drive the other person away.

It is understandable that a person from such a background might have a fear of abandonment or loss and want the security of a regular paycheck and retirement plan as opposed to career risk taking. They, like Marcus, are looking for someone or something to make them feel protected and secure. No relationship or job can ever offer such security. The unconscious program of security and survival leaves one with the feeling that something is always missing and if that "something" was present, one would be happy, safe, and so on. There is a pervasive, existential anxiety regarding loss that is sometimes experienced as a "knot" in the chest or stomach. This fear goes beyond just a concern for disconnection with others but can also involve a sense of loss of self, a disconnection from our own hearts.

This unconscious program for happiness presents as a fear of aloneness and disconnection. There is a fundamental aloneness that is necessary to be all right with oneself in this world. The challenge is how to be at home with ourselves when such aloneness feels like persecution. People like

Marcus do not experience their aloneness in any sort of meditative or peaceful way. During times of being alone, the mind spins precariously with thoughts of uncertainty such as, *What will happen next?* or *Can I trust this person?* or *Am I missing some vital piece of information?*

We want others to take away our fears. For example, someone might think, *If he/she will pay attention to me, then my loneliness will go away.* If the person from whom attention is being sought is preoccupied or not interested, this can lead to the feeling of abandonment. Methods to gain attention are often anxiety based and impulsive and can cause further damage to an already strained relationship.

Trying to meet life's needs through others, people like Marcus strive to fulfill their illusion of a need for relevance and effectiveness. Ultimately, the only way to transcend the loneliness is to accept being alone, invite it in, and not reject it. The loneliness exists in the form of energy in our bodies that has been repressed over and over again. We must feel this energy and take responsibility for our fears. In order to form genuine intimacy, we must first overcome our neediness and fear of aloneness. (Chapters 6 and 7 will lead you through the process of letting go of this repressed energy.)

A communication from Bill Wilson, cofounder of Alcoholics Anonymous, written in January 1958 and entitled "The Next Frontier: Emotional Sobriety" speaks of this fear of security and survival. Bill said, "Suddenly I realized what the matter was. My basic flaw had always been dependence—almost absolute dependence—on people or circumstances to supply me with prestige, security, and the like. Failing to get these things according to my perfectionistic dreams and specifications, I had fought for them. And when defeat came so did my depression." As Bill Wilson states so well, he was dependent on others to meet his emotional needs for a personal sense of security, but this is a losing formula, because the only one who can make one all right is the person himself. Any program that depends on external validation will produce insecurity.

Affection and Esteem

This unconscious value system for happiness feels like a roller-coaster ride. Life is determined by the "show" that is put on for others. If they like it and tell me that I'm wonderful, then I am all right. If it doesn't work, I am devastated. People with this type of lifestyle grew up in families where there was no unconditional love. They were loved conditionally, and guilt was a favored teaching tool: *If the only way I can earn your love is to be perfect, I am doomed to fail.*

In a child, this is experienced as an emotional split between prohibition and fantasy. Prohibition consists of the internalized parental injunction "You are not good enough," causing the child to have a pervasive sense of guilt and perfectionism that cannot be reconciled. Fantasy comes into play as a mechanism of survival.

Life is difficult when you are always looking for someone or something to validate you. One might join an organization or do volunteer work as a way to seek appreciation or to be seen as a "good person." Sometimes, this person will spend an inordinate amount of time telling others about all of the good things he/she has accomplished, hoping for admiration. Living this kind of life certainly has the ups and downs of a carnival ride.

The unconscious program for happiness regarding affection and esteem comes from a basic fear of unworthiness. This can lead to the creation of a narcissistic, grandiose core as a compensation for hurt and isolation. When one believes he/she can "never measure up," a fantasy world develops that precludes true connection and bonding to others. The ego lives by comparison, contrast, and competition. *I am only all right if I am better than you. I must have a nicer car, a bigger home, or anything that makes me look good on the outside.* This comes across as arrogance but is essentially a cover-up for the hurt and loneliness experienced on the inside. People with this program really want to be liked but tend to push others away with the cover-up. The "neediness" within has no idea how to ask for loving connection or help.

Feeling generally inadequate and unworthy of love, it seems that no matter what one does, it never really fulfills the internal desire of just wanting to be all right with the world— to have true friends and to feel comfortable in one's own skin. This inadequacy leads to forcefully proving ourselves through workaholism or other realms of overachievement. The only other alternative is to give up entirely. These two extremes reinforce the basic fear of unworthiness.

I understand this unconscious program very well. For most of my life, it was my story. My father was a cardiologist who was a workaholic. His absence from my early life spoke tons about how I interpreted his love for me. When someone doesn't show up for your school plays or your Little League or midget football games, it speaks of your value to them. Yet, at the same time, my father was my hero. He saved many patients and was extremely well respected in our community. He truly loved his patients, as well as medicine. I believed that I could never be as good as he was, but for much of my early life I tried, measuring my value against my illusion of my father's success and thereby setting myself up for failure.

Mercilessly self-judging, I created unachievable standards for myself. When I started teaching more than thirty years ago, my greatest fear was that someone would ask a question that I could not answer. This threatened my projected self-image of who I was supposed to be and, at the same time, confirmed my negative belief that I was unworthy. For people like me, failure felt fatal. Before I began growing spiritually, there were so many times that I just wanted to give up.

Power and Control

Imagine growing up in a home where you felt totally power-less over your environment and life, and any effort at extending your personal boundaries was thwarted. During this time, when the child is first learning to be productive through the use of his/her physical and intellectual capabilities, a parent, caregiver, or older sibling generally plays a very domineering role. The danger of this domineering family member is that the child may develop a sense of inferiority and inadequacy, despairing about the potency of his/her tools and skills. One way to compensate for such a situation when one grows up is to become that which stifled him/her to begin with. Out of fear, he/she desperately tries to control people and situations. Since controlling others is impossible, this leads to suffering, as plans that are intended to bring happiness continuously fail. In order to deal with the failure, the ego wants to blame everything on the other person or situation.

Rage may temporarily provide someone with a feeling of power and control, but it will eventually destroy relationships. Constantly worrying about a situation is yet another attempt at control. (Worry can be defined as a person's negative thoughts about a future event.) Excessive or chronic worry operates under the misperception that our thinking is enhanced as we try to control every situation. Unfortunately, cognitive processing is hindered and overstimulation of emotional and fear processes take place. As an example of this, consider that you are being called into your immediate supervisor's office at work and you do not know why. Your mind may immediately come up with many possibilities—mostly negative—and then, in order to create the illusion of control, may come up with the actual statements you are going to say to your supervisor to counter any possible negative perception on his/her part. All of these ruminations rarely have anything to do with what will actually happen in the meeting. In reality, you may actually be getting a small increase in your salary and/or a promotion.

I once had a client who struggled mightily with two female executives who were just above her in the organizational hierarchy of a large company. She was a very intelligent youngest child who never seemed to get her way when she was young. She became controlling and demanding in her relationship with her older sisters, and these same attributes were causing her difficulty in her work life. Since the two senior executives had similar issues, every time Marsha sat in the meeting room, there was generally a battle of egos that was, at times, quite nasty. Obviously, Marsha, the junior executive, did not fare well in these meetings and came to me to decide whether she should leave the company or stick it out.

The problem for people like Marsha is that there are millions of people in the world with the same power and control issues. They want to dictate what will happen in every situation and cannot be "happy" unless they succeed. When they lose, they experience great grief, anger, and despair. However, they project the problem on to the other person. The ego says, "That person doesn't know what is good for the company (or himself/herself). He/she should listen to me because I know what is best." The ego always externalizes the bad to protect itself.

These people suffer from a fear of losing safety and control. There is an element of generalized anxiety disorder, as it is often accompanied by the belief that "If I don't control things, something bad will happen." Those whose lives are affected by illusions of power and control often tend to have a very linear approach to life. When you speak with them about nonlinear, subjective spirituality, they dismiss it as something they already understand or something that doesn't really matter. This is because the nonlinear cannot be controlled. They might be deeply religious, hanging on to the dogma of the church, but the spiritual realm is a source of great anxiety since it cannot be seen, felt, or controlled. Uncertainty and insecurity are the result.

When they do not get their way—whether real or perceived—a strong negative emotional response is triggered. This is the old animal brain signaling that they are in dangerous and insecure territory. Imagined fears of being criticized or concern about what they may be doing wrong creates great suffering and misery.

The Prefrontal Cortex

In order to understand the ego's programs for happiness, an understanding of the development of the prefrontal cortex (PFC) is necessary. New brain imaging techniques have allowed us to know more about the PFC. Under ideal circumstances, the PFC takes about twenty-five years to fully form. During the time from around age two until ten (every child varies as these are just average ages based on personal observation and understanding of developmental psychology and neurobiology), the brain does not have self-reflective capacity. The PFC is a perfect recording machine. It records what it hears and sees and even what it doesn't hear or see (like a father not showing up for a Little League game) as relative absolutes. The brain is concrete in its operations and doesn't interpret or analyze at that age. When it hears "Don't be so stupid" or "What is wrong with you?" it internalizes "I am stupid" and "Something is wrong with me." Over time, it is not hard to imagine the child believing that everything he/she does is wrong and that he/she is fundamentally flawed.

As it matures, the PFC allows us to abstract, conceptualize, and analyze life situations, but these abilities do not develop until around ages ten to sixteen. This is also when the brain develops the ability to ask questions regarding what is being said and done to determine if something is in one's best interest or not. At this point, a child can look at what is happening and determine right from wrong. They have the capacity for self-reflective consciousness. For example, at age twelve Marcus could see that what his father was doing to him was wrong. He probably noticed that his friends' fathers were not physically abusing their sons. At age twelve, Marcus made the decision to never let his father hurt him again. It is around this age that many people with histories of early-life developmental trauma make the decision to not let anyone hurt them again. Marcus discovered when he got into people's faces in an angry, rage-filled fashion, he could get them to back off. Unfortunately, these repetitive reactions ended with his being fired and thrown into jail. Other ten- to sixteen-year-olds may run away from home, cut or burn themselves, or turn to alcohol, drugs, food, or sex for escape.

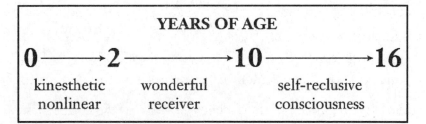

FIGURE 2.2. Here we see the developmental trajectory of the prefrontal cortex in early life. I believe the first two years are feeling oriented and nonlinear. Year two until around ten is a more concrete time when the brain takes in information from its environment in a literal fashion. Around age two, we develop our separate selves and become "me." Finally, during the time frame of ten until around sixteen, the brain develops self-reflective consciousness necessary for abstraction and the ability to analyze veracity.

During early life, we all experience some level of developmental difficulty leading to repression of frustrating or painful experiences into the unconscious mind or the development of compensatory attitudes and behaviors. The ego is developed to compensate for the pain of unfulfilled instinctual needs. It is not until between ages ten and sixteen that we develop reflective self-consciousness, which allows us to question and doubt the messages of early life.

Remember the ego's value systems for happiness: *security and survival, affection and esteem,* and *power and control.* The ego and its programs were learned from our families, religion, culture, environment, and so on. Literally, the more we are controlled by the ego and these programs for happiness, the fewer personal choices we have. It is difficult to believe that so much of our lives is guided by others whose teachings and behavior we incorporated into what has been defined as the "real self." But the ego is not who we are. We will only be free to serve a higher purpose when we discover that which we truly are—when we remember our true Self or our souls, the essence of who we really are. Before we get there, however, it is important to thoroughly understand the cunning and baffling nature of our egos and the forces of desire and pride that serve as the motor and the front man for the ego.

From the Self, the "small self" or ego emerges very early in life. When the small child perceives the other (mother) as separate from the self, the ego is born. This activates life on the linear level (level of duality), as there is now *you* and there is *me.* The story of Adam and Eve gives us an approximate metaphor. They

lived in the nonlinear world but were tempted by the first duality—the understanding of the polarities of good and evil—in the
form of the Tree of Knowledge of Good and Evil. When they ate
of the fruit, they fell into the linear world where "oneness" is lost
and dualities abide. To apply the consequences of story to the
entire human race, our differences are now exposed, and we
need to hide ourselves in shame. The ego now calls itself "me" or
"I." There is an *us* and a *them*. We are right and they are wrong.
Any differences between us are perceived as threats to our egos.

Think about this for a few moments. This is the origin of
blame, racism, prejudice, judgmentalism, and other perceptions that have destroyed not only the lives of humans but of
entire nations and races. The goal of the spiritual search is to
move back into the nonlinear realm of existence. The goal is true
happiness, but the ego doesn't know where to find it. According
to Saint Augustine's theology of original sin, the consequences
of the separation of our true selves from our egos are:

- Illusion: We don't know what true happiness is or where
  to find it.
- Concupiscence: We are made for happiness but try to find
  it in all of the wrong places.
- Weakness of will: Even if we discovered what and where
  true happiness lies, the will is too weak to do anything
  about it.

The fact of the matter is our will is too weak to recover from the suffering caused by the ego's unconscious programs for happiness. We emotionally react to people, places, and things. We judge everything by "Is it good for my instinctual programs for happiness or not?" We continually ask, "Is it safe?" "Can I control this?" and "Am I all right?" And, finally, we expect other people and circumstances to meet our own personal needs by making us feel safe, in control, and okay.

I watch small children play hide-and-seek with the world while warmly held by a loving parent. If they can catch your eye, the game begins. They look over their parents' shoulders and play peekaboo with you. When they see you looking at them, they duck back into the safety of the parent's chest. This must be the primordial game of all humankind. We come out and show a little of ourselves only to duck back inside when we feel a little too exposed and vulnerable. In order to achieve happiness, we must expose the pride and other character defects of the ego. There may be no more difficult task than to see our egos as they really are—egocentric, grandiose, self-serving, and afraid. It usually requires a teacher (verbal or written) to serve as a mirror reflecting back to us the mechanics of our egos as it is often not apparent to us without help.

As I've mentioned, the brain is a receiver that is programmed by early-life experiences and messages from family, community, religion, and culture. We call this programming the basis of the ego. This programming is also the basis for our character defects. We could say that the ego and character defects are synonymous. We learn that the road to Self is not about trying to acquire anything but the willingness to surrender all of this egoic programming and thus take ourselves back to that which we are—the Self, or God immanent.

What are character defects? Some might describe these defects in terms of the seven deadly sins: greed, anger, lust, pride, envy, gluttony, and sloth or procrastination. There is a gentler way to look at the defects. For example, one can ask such questions as:

> *Have I been so proud that I've been scorned (disrespected)*
> *as a braggart (bragger)?*
> *Have I acted pridefully, consciously or unconsciously,*
> *out of fear?*
> *Do I like to feel and act superior to others?*
> *Have I been so greedy that I've been or could be labeled a thief?*
> *Do I long for the possessions of others out of fear of not getting*
> *enough?*
> *Do I let greed masquerade as ambition?*
> *Do I get angry out of fear when my instinctive demands are*
> *threatened?*
> *Have I enjoyed self-righteous anger in the fact that many*
> *people annoy me and that makes me superior to them?*
> *Have I enjoyed gossiping as a polite form of murder by*
> *character assassination?*
> *Do I grab for everything I can, fearing I'll never have enough?*
> *Do I bury myself in my work, hobbies, or activities?*

Do I suffer from never being satisfied with what I have?
Have I spent more time wishing for what others have
*   than working toward getting what I want?*
Do I loaf and procrastinate?
Do I work grudgingly and under half steam? [9]

These simple but profound questions are keys that can open the door to ourselves. Being human, we have egos. Our egos are the source of our defects of character. Our defects of character are the source of our suffering.

In this chapter, I revealed some of the reasons why our lives become miserable and unmanageable. The ego is the source of all suffering and misery in life. In the next chapter, I will continue to develop the illusion called the ego. We will see how the pride of the ego can become so powerful that we cannot even view the Self. In other words, we completely lose our true Self and, in the process, become what our caregivers and environmental influences tell us we are. Once we have gained a thorough working knowledge of the ego, we can discuss how we can counteract and/or alleviate the ego's control over us. This is a choice you will have to make. Are you ready to take the risk of changing your life? Are you ready to take the responsibility for becoming that which you are destined to be? It is a narrow road, but one filled with ultimate discovery and beauty. Everything is already yours. All you have to do is realize and accept your Divine birthright.

---

[9] Twelve Steps and Twelve Traditions. AA World Services. NY, NY, 2003, pgs 48,49,66,67.

3

My Ego Loves Nobody, Including Me

"Why do you see the splinter in your brother's eye, and do not see the beam in your own eye?" [10]

—Jesus speaking in the Gospel of Luke

---

[10] St. Luke 6:41, *Holy Bible*, trans. George M. Lamsa.

Why is it we can always see everyone else's problems so clearly but are virtually blind to our own? We always seem to be the last to know. Rather than continue to wait, we can take a fearless and searching personal inventory of ourselves now and develop a perspective about our current state of affairs. The pressing questions that must be asked are *How did it get this way?* and *What can I do to make things better?*

Everything we experience in this world is processed in, and takes place in, our brains. Could it be that nothing is as it seems and our experiences are just figments of our imaginations? Our sensations may feel accurate and full of truth, but they do not necessarily represent the reality of the outside world. Moreover, the neural mechanisms that account for what we believe to be reality are also responsible for our dreams, lapses in memory, and delusions (an invalid set of beliefs). *The Diagnostic and Statistical Manual of Mental Disorders* (DSM-IV) defines a delusion as "an erroneous belief that usually involves a misinterpretation of perceptions or experiences."[11] But you certainly don't have to have a mental disorder to misinterpret things. So if reality is a neurobiological illusion, and "I" and "me" are names for my ego, and the ego is not who I really am, then who am I? *This* is the journey we are undertaking.

We live in a world disordered by the words "I" and "me." The top spiritual problem in our culture is the lie of individu-

---

[11] *Diagnostic and Statistical Manual of Mental Disorders,* 4th ed.. (Washington, DC: American Psychiatric Association, 1994), 275.

alism. How isolating and depressing it is to believe that one is totally alone and beyond assistance and completely dependent upon oneself to figure this world out. It wasn't so long ago that I existed in the bitterness of a world I thought I'd created for myself. Sitting here now, writing this, these words take me back to a time when I felt so alone, and I sink into my seat with great sorrow, wondering how I or anyone else could feel so blue and lost in this magnificent world.

To see and touch the big mystery called the kingdom of God by Jesus, Enlightenment by Buddha, and the Truth by myriad philosophers provided me with a firm foundation in God and a solid point of reference, allowing me to ask, *What does this teach me?* It can do that for you too. Sadly, there are still many whose reference point changes based on the next commercial and whose fragile self-image is threatened with every discussion. It's like "the pinball theory of life," where they bounce from one thing to the next and from high to low, attributing the highs to themselves and blaming the lows on others, never moving, never changing, and not even paying attention.

How many times have you heard variations of the following statements?

> *"I know exactly what to do!"* (Ignorance)
> *"I want that . . . and that."* (Greed)
> *"I have a right to that."* (Entitlement)
> *"I can't believe he/she did that!"* (Resentment)
> *"Compared to him/her, I don't have enough."* (Envy)

*"**I** am more competent than him/her."* (Pride)

*"**I** didn't get my share of that."* (Jealousy)

No wonder people feel so tired and out of sorts with life! What they don't seem to understand is that *I* and *me* are just temporary states that represent the ego, which can never be satisfied. The ego is so busy worrying about itself and what's missing from its life that it doesn't allow us to see what's there. Fortunately, because the ego is a transient illusion, it *can* be deflated during this life, leaving room for us to cultivate our true, eternal being: the Self. The Self cannot be deflated, because it is not in the game of win or lose. The Self just eternally is!

Using Thomas Merton as a guide, one can look at the ego in the following manner: " we too easily assume that we are our real selves, and that our choices are really the ones we want to make when, in fact, our acts of free choice are (though morally imputable, no doubt) largely dictated by psychological compulsions, flowing from our inordinate ideas of our own importance. Our choices are too often dictated by our false selves."[12] Merton has such a beautiful way of getting right to the point. Our egos are making the decisions and asking what is good for us and not what the best decision for everyone involved is. The Self will always choose what it believes to be the best choice for humankind.

---

[12] Merton, *No Man Is an Island*, 25.

What Is Self-Love?

The commandment "Love thy neighbor as thyself" presupposes that one loves himself/herself. But what is self-love? Self-love is neither self-centeredness nor selfishness. (These are actually forms of self-hatred.) Self-love is unconditional self-acceptance and self-caring. The ego's "love" for itself is not self-love. Its excessively solicitous nature regarding "me" is not love, but rather delusional and selfish prejudice. *My ego loves nobody—and that includes me!* The ego is dualistic. It "loves" one part of you but hates others. The "love" of the ego is truly conditional. *I will love you if you do this for me, but not if you don't.* Love-hate relationships have nothing to do with love, other than that they cheapen it. Self-love is true love. It is love of the Self.

I have been writing about the ego as if it were an entirely negative force, but this isn't the case. At lower levels of spiritual consciousness, the ego dominates, causing shame, guilt, pride, hate, and other feelings that lead to much suffering, but its existence serves a purpose. The ego was born out of the need to acquire energy for survival from outside ourselves (unlike plants, which do not have to seek energy due to photosynthesis). We needed to learn what was dangerous and what wasn't, what we could befriend and what would eat us if it got close enough, what would kill us if we ate it and what was good to eat.

Looking at it this way, the ego's principle of self-interest and survival makes great practical sense and established the ego's main core, which is primarily involved in self-interest, acquisition, conquest, and competition for survival. Also on the positive side, the ego is curious, always searching and learning. Without these characteristics, the spiritual search would be improbable. Therefore, the annihilation of the ego is not the end goal. Rather, the ego is compassionately dissolved back into its source—the Self.

The Self is all about the truth and seeing the essence of what is really going on. It is easy to conceive a role for the ego here. We would have been in dire straits—especially during our early years when we lacked self-reflective skills—if we had to deal with all of the dysfunction around us without any way to escape from such reality. In situations such as early-life developmental trauma, the role of the ego is a grace.

Unfortunately, as we get older, these same ego defenses that helped us as children make it difficult for us to climb the mountain leading to truth and Self. The Self is hidden behind the clouds of the ego. The energy level is so low that one might feel helpless and shamed. (Shame is a gross undervaluation of one's self. Its energy level is even below that of the self-centered narcissist.) Moreover, the ego is judgmental. It compares and competes with everyone and against everything. It is the source of existential anxiety and depression. We truly miss out on life as all the good things go right by while we are trying to figure out if we are better or worse than, richer or poorer than, the new family on the block.

The ego treats everything and everyone as an object to be manipulated, feared, cultivated, hated, or possessed. It fails to see the humanity in another. Contrarily, being able to identify with others and to see them as human beings with similar struggles and anxieties creates a unique intersubjective experience of "oneness." From this mustard seed of humanity, we can start to develop the small and large branches that reveal the oneness that connects us to everything.

The ego vacillates between the past and the future and is driven by fear: fear that we will not be good enough; fear that we will not be loved and thus abandoned and alienated; fear that we are powerless over everything. The ego sees humility and surrender as weaknesses and reliance on anything outside of itself as a "sucker's play." It milks every situation. It can be the consummate victim: *Everybody is screwing me over.* Or it can be the consummate perpetrator: *I did this to you because you need to be taught a lesson.* In fact, the ego can be anything that suits its purpose, because it is the consummate chameleon. However, it is not the one thing it really wants to be—and that is God.

The ego loves the dynamic tension of life—its motives and schemes and character flaws. It loves to compete for praise, power, and love, and this makes it dishonest. There is a possessive and insatiable desire to control others and accumulate wealth. The ego trusts only itself, seeking only its own needs and self-gratifications.

It is very hard to live like this, especially with the "should haves" and the "ought to be's" driving the chatter in the left hemispheres of our brains (more on this in Chapter 9). The reward center in our brains and mass-media advertising are the perfect foils for the ego. The nucleus accumbens and ventral tegmental areas (VTAs) of the midbrain comprise a part of a system referred to as the "reward center" or "seeking system." The seeking system is involved in high anticipation, intense interest, and insatiable curiosity. Often the most arresting part is the hunt itself. It is a neuroemotional system driving and energizing the many complexities of human experience, such as persistent feelings of interest, sensation seeking, and curiosity, and in the presence of the highly complex cortex, the search for higher meaning.

Advertisements highlight the higher narcissistic meanings of life. They tell the ego that we cannot be respected without driving a certain brand of automobile, or we can't be intimate sexually without a drug, or that "clothes makes the man/woman." The ego tries to keep us convinced that we need to look everywhere for the answers with the exception of inside ourselves.

The requirement to live instead of just survive is to be free of the ego rather than going from one egoic notion of freedom to another, for the latter is just a sideways movement into another attachment, often referred to as "switching addictions." When our energy is diverted from the love of God, Self, and meaningful others, an attachment or addiction takes place. Material things can rust, break, or be stolen. They do not last. Misery and suffering are the result.

Let's step back for a moment and try to reconcile our notions about the ego. In Western psychology, the ego is given great importance as a structure that allows us to be able to act in an adultlike fashion. In other words, this ego allows us to be able to inhibit primitive impulses and urges. From an Eastern spiritual perspective (the perspective I have used in writing this book), the ego is often viewed as an illusion. I would endeavor to reconcile these apparent opposing views by saying that the ego and its defenses are very valuable to children growing up, as I previously mentioned, especially if they live in a world of chaos, which many do. Psychology speaks of defenses, scripts, or schemata that help us get through some of what we are ill prepared to deal with as children. However, as we get older, these ways of thinking may not work for us at all and may be very harmful to establishing good relationships with others, both professionally and personally.

So part of growing up, then, is to rid ourselves of these childish, narcissistic ways. This is the spiritual journey, and it involves a dramatic change in intention. The egoic "What's in it for me?" notion is replaced by unconditional love (or serenity) and integrity.

Pride: The Core of the Ego

The core of the ego is pride. This is not to say that all forms of personal pride are flawed. Self-worth (good self-esteem) is secondary to effort and achievement. It is earned. In regard to egoic pride, real worth is not a consideration. The genesis of pride is entitlement coming from unresolved infantile narcissistic egocentricity (self-centeredness). This type of entitlement produces a lack of remorse and all resentments are justified. One can even develop a spiritual pride that makes it okay to hold a "better than" attitude and cast negative judgment onto others.

Pride can also be perceived as a spiritual defect, the basis of sin and the core of evil in the world. There is a refusal to surrender to God and an overall arrogance applied to personal thoughts and beliefs. In life you run into those who spend all their time telling others how to think and behave even in circumstances in which they have no experience.

Pride is a great defense against the vulnerabilities and inherent weaknesses of the ego. Just imagine how much energy it takes to protect yourself from the "slings and arrows" of those trying to chop you off at the knees. The arrogance of pride creates the need to constantly show and tell others how great you are. By implication, this means that everyone else is inferior to you. These types of traits are manageable in small children but are very unbecoming in adults.

Pride is the true front man for the ego. It filters all input such that everything is perceived from the entitled perspective of the ego. It is all about "me." Pride keeps us from a glimpse of Self, inflates denial, and doesn't allow us to acknowledge our defects of character.

Desire

We all seem to have some degree of desire for something outside of ourselves that we think will somehow make us all right. I remember when I thought, *If I can just get that master's degree, I will be happy.* Then it was the doctorate. I earned both degrees, but they didn't make me any happier. Instead, I felt more disillusioned. Then I had to have a certain type of job, but that didn't make me happy either. Desire comes from some sense of "lack." There is something missing within. As so eloquently stated by my late friend Tom Brady, it's "like a hole in the middle, and when the cold wind blows, it hurts." The ego promises us relief from this ache, and this is the ego's Achilles' heel. We continue to go further and further into our habits with alcohol, drugs, food, gambling, sex, and so on to try to fill this hole, and we ultimately fail.

Maybe the most treacherous aspect of desire is that sex, gambling, drugs, alcohol, and so on get us close to that feeling of being connected, of being just okay, but we can never possess it and it never lasts. Over time the "sweet spot" gets harder and harder to hit as dependence and tolerance—with all the nasty, toxic side effects—begin to win the struggle. We got so close to achieving that feeling of sheer Self, that we will chase that experience for the rest of our using days. Money, personal extravagances, and other possessions can have a similar effect. As novelist Thomas Wolfe writes in *Look Homeward, Angel*, "In all the earth there was no other like him, no other fitted to be so sublimely and magnificently drunken . . . Why, when it was possible to buy a God in a bottle, and drink him off, and become a God oneself, were men not forever drunken?"[13] Wolfe is speaking of how alcohol caused a temporary sense of connectedness to the God within (which I have been calling the Self).

There is another side to desire. Spirituality can be seen as a response to our very human sense of incompleteness. The core of spirituality can be felt as a haunting sense of incompleteness, a yearning for completion—uncertainty craving certainty and brokenness in need of wholeness. Yearning is a desire to love and be loved as God loves us. Therefore, desire is at the core of our spiritual quest. It is a burning energy for that which promises to bring us closer to the eternal—to completion, certainty, and wholeness, and to allow us to connect with that which is most life-giving. The spiritual quest has a lot to do with how we handle this thirst or yearning. When we search for completeness by using alcohol, drugs, work, gambling, food, and/or sex, it is not the search itself that is wrong, but the

---

[13] Thomas Wolfe, *Look Homeward, Angel: A Story of Buried Life* (New York: Charles Scribner's Sons, 1947), 525.

methods we are using to try to fulfill what those things never can. Unfortunately, we often go too far and get caught up in addiction or other negative dependencies. So where do we go from here?

We stand at the crossroads of decision. Which way will it be? Will we succumb to the old ways of the ego or are we brave enough to try something radically new? It takes no courage at all to repeat failure. At a certain point it gets comfortable, and we start expecting it of ourselves. There is another way. For example, as the Big Book of Alcoholics Anonymous states, "Rarely have we seen a person fail who has thoroughly followed our path. Those who do not recover are people who cannot or will not completely give themselves to this simple program, usually men and women constitutionally incapable of being honest with themselves."[14]

As with any spiritual path such as Alcoholics Anonymous, radical honesty with oneself is the necessary starting point of the journey. This is when one admits to oneself the exact nature of their wrongdoings—and so begins the struggle. Cherokee wisdom discusses this struggle in the lesson of the Two Wolves:

> One evening an old Cherokee told his grandson about a battle that goes on inside people.
>
> "My son," he began, "the battle is between two 'wolves' inside us all. One is evil. It is anger, envy, jealousy, sorrow,

---

[14] *Alcoholics Anonymous*, 3rd ed. (New York: Alcoholics Anonymous World Services, 1976), 58.

regret, greed, arrogance, self-pity, guilt, resentment, inferiority, lies, false pride, superiority, and ego. The other is good. It is joy, peace, love, hope, serenity, humility, kindness, benevolence, empathy, generosity, truth, compassion, and faith."

The grandson thought for a moment, then asked, "Which wolf wins the battle, Grandfather?" And the old Cherokee replied, "The one you feed."

I believe the ego's formation of resentments—the belief that someone or something is wronging us—is the leading reason for our self-destructive behaviors. Whether it is a relapse to alcohol and/or drugs, sloughing off work responsibilities, acting out in relationships, or just downright becoming self-destructive, resentments allow us to abdicate personal responsibility. We fool ourselves into believing other people or situations have the ability to cause us to misbehave or feel negative emotions. In reality, no person or thing can *make* us feel angry, anxious, or depressed except ourselves, and no one can make us misbehave but us.

We become occupied by so much fear. Life becomes increasingly difficult to live as we internalize the energy of our unresolved grief and anguish. If we could only learn to accept ourselves as we are—our physical bodies without shame and our emotions without becoming overwhelmed with envy and guilt—we would understand that there is little or nothing to fear in life. Our only possible fears would be the species' specific and genetically encoded, unconscious negative responses. As Elisabeth Kübler-Ross states:

> *Most important of all, we must learn to love and be loved unconditionally. Most of us have been raised as prostitutes. I will love you "if." And this word "if" has ruined and destroyed more lives than anything else on planet earth. It prostitutes us; it makes us feel that we can buy love with good behavior, or good grades. We will never develop a sense of self-love and self-reward. If we were not able to accommodate the grown-ups, we were punished, rather than being taught by consistent loving discipline. As our teachers taught, if you had been raised with unconditional love and discipline you will never be afraid of the windstorms of life. You would have no fear, no guilt and no anxieties, the only enemies of men. Should you shield the canyon from the windstorms you would never see the beauty of their carvings.*[15]

The ego has a narcissistic core that desires personal gain and is grandiose and prideful in its worldview. Grandiosity is a way of looking at the world. It says, "In order for me to be all right, I must be better than you." On the inside is loneliness and isolation, but the outside is a front for the world to see. In order to be okay, I must have the best things—and the most—and when my ship comes in, I will show you all how great I am. For example, an addict named James bragged to me about all

---

[15] Elisabeth Kübler-Ross, *On Life After Death* (Berkeley, CA: Celestial Arts, 1991), 63–64.

the money he made selling drugs and all the drugs he consumed. I found this particularly revealing as he stood in front of me in a treatment setting, as it was the choice he made as opposed to going to jail. He was just standing there in front of me without the proverbial pot to urinate in. One is left to say, "What is wrong with this picture?" To say it is transparent is to state the case only mildly. James ultimately relapsed and ended up in jail.

More often than not, our minds want us to believe that the past "should not" have been the way it was and that we do not deserve what the past gave to us or what the future may hold. Our minds reflect over and over how it should have been, or it takes us on a journey into a future we could never predict.

Think of your brain as a piece of hardware, somewhat like a personal computer. Hardware serves as a wonderful receiver for external programming. Imagine all of the messages you received early in life about who you are, who to like and dislike, what is right and what is wrong, and what you are supposed to be when you grow up as software that is constantly being uploaded into your brain. This software is the ego. Another way to think of the ego is as clouds in the sky. The Self is the sun that is always there behind the clouds. The clouds are the shades that block your ability to see the sun. As the clouds break apart and begin to move away, the sun or "that which you are," shines through.

The spiritual search involves discovering and removing

each piece of software or cloud. You do not need to add a thing. You already have it all. This is so difficult for the part of us that must acquire or own things—the ego—to deal with, as it is so used to going out and getting something to relieve a perceived deficit.

Origins of Human Misery and Suffering

For I do not know what I do; and I do not do the thing which I want, but I do the thing which I hate. That is exactly what I do. So then if I do that which I do not wish to do, I can testify concerning the law that is good. Now then it is not I who do it but sin which dominates me. Yet I know that it does not fully dominate me (that is in my flesh); but as far as good is concerned, the choice is easy for me to make, but to do it is difficult to me. For it is not the good that I wish to do, that I do; but it is the evil that I do not wish to do, that I do. Now if I do that which I do not wish, then it is not I who do it, but the sin which dominates me. I find therefore that the law agrees with my conscience when I wish to do good, but evil is always near, distracting me. For I delight in the law of God after the inward man; But I see another law in my members, warring against the law of my mind, and it makes me captive to the law of sin which is in my members.

O wretched man that I am! Who shall deliver me from this mortal body?[16]

---

[16] Romans 7:15–24, *Holy Bible*, trans. George M. Lamsa.

Like the apostle Paul in the preceding scripture, life has given me numerous occasions to reflect on the sources of my misery. Life has also led me to a number of other people from whom I have been grateful to learn. When I reflect upon the many clients I have worked with who suffered from depression, anxiety, rage, or addiction, there seems to be some consistent themes regarding their existence. There seems to be four distinct areas of egoic functioning that are principal contributors to the misery and emotional suffering bound to the human condition. By understanding and bringing into consciousness these aspects of our being, we can make decisions about whether we want to change or not. These areas are:

1. The belief that our personality is the essence of who we are.
2. The belief that happiness is found outside of ourselves.
3. The inability to remain consciously in this moment.
4. The importance given to personal and material attachments.

The Belief That Our Personality Is the Essence of Who We Are

In my experience, people who seek help for any number of life problems usually use negative words to describe themselves. Hearing statements such as "Everything I do is always wrong" and "Why does all this bad stuff happen to me?" makes it easy to see how people can become overwhelmed by their negative beliefs about who they are. However, the answer to the question "Is that really who you are?" is, I believe, an emphatic "No, it is not!"

The Hindu spiritual path Advaita Vedanta states that there is only one real or true thing in the universe. Everything else is "maya"—an illusion. This one real thing is called Atman. Atman is the soul, or what I have been referring to as the Self. The real thing is also called Brahman. Brahman is God. The soul, Self, or Atman is the same thing as God or Brahman. God is within us and is the essence of who we are. Beneath all of the personality structures, opinions, obnoxious behaviors, and inability to see the current state of affairs clearly (denial and other psychological defense strategies) is the true Self, the gift of God, the life force breathed into Adam. This is who we really are. Every spiritual journey moves us back toward the essence of Self.

It takes incredible understanding and compassion to see the love and beauty inside such unlovely creatures who are so full of anger, hate, and self-pity. People with advanced spiritual consciousness by their sheer presence are able to reduce the pain and shame of the other and allow for the process of healing to commence. As a person successfully engages in a spiritual program, his/her true Self shines through. Once the person starts to develop compassion for himself/herself, he/she can start to help others who cannot see any personal, redeeming qualities within themselves. It is true: the healed becomes the healer. With escalating spiritual consciousness comes compassion for self and the gift of healing energy to be shared with others.

The Belief That Happiness Is Found Outside of Ourselves

How many times in your life have you said things like, "When I finish school, I'll be happy," "If I buy that car everyone will admire me, and I'll be happy," "If I can just get that promotion and make more money, I'll be happy," or "When I get married and start a family, I'll be happy"? If it was as simple as that, we would all be a lot "happier" than we are.

The above are just the empty promises of the ego, which is constantly looking outside of itself to live up to its promises to us. *Do this, and you will be all right. Take that drug, and it will make you happy.* It is this ego that is constantly comparing us to everyone else. It is narcissistic and can only be "happy" if it has more and better toys than anyone else. In order to feel good on the inside, it believes it is necessary to have things from the outside. The ego believes that happiness is external. It is the new car. It is the new house. It is found in drugs, sex, clothing, and possessions.

Above all, what the ego seeks is not real happiness at all. The ego's world is one of illusion fed by the media and marketing industry. As mentioned in the Introduction and in Chapter 2, it is all about the ego's programs for happiness: *security and survival, affection and esteem, power and control.* Grandiosity leads us to constant comparisons to those around us. In order to be happy, I must have bigger, better, more expensive toys so that I can feel good about myself. He/she who lives only to accumulate the most toys before he dies is already dead.

This rather self-critical and perfectionistic aspect of the ego never really allows us to enjoy what we have accomplished, as there must be more and better on top of more and better that will ultimately make us supremely happy. Unfortunately, it often takes a life disaster to lead us toward humility and the understanding that external things are nice but not important. Instead of putting our energies into the acquisition of material things, we learn that "resting in God" and doing God's work with gratitude on this earth is where true happiness resides. It is in the giving of ourselves that we find out who we really are and what we were meant to be in this world. Unconditional love is the source of our serenity.

The Inability to Remain Consciously in This Moment

Most people are preoccupied with the past and the future. Suffering increases as we move away from the present. Techniques such as mindfulness meditation teach us how to be at peace in the moment without distractions from the past or worry about the future. Mindfulness is not trying to change anything. Rather, it involves observing the mind, body, and emotions just the way they are. In other words, mindfulness allows us to "be" in the moment.

However, the other choice, when we are not mindful, is to be on automatic pilot or in a state of unawareness. In this state of unawareness, we spend energy daydreaming, anticipating the future, worrying about the past, or fantasizing. This is the ego at work. When we are unaware, we engage in the pure insanity of life, which is doing the same thing over and over again but expecting the results to be different.

Time is a man-made concept that exists as a linear reference point. Using this reference point, we can divide time into the past, the present, and the future.

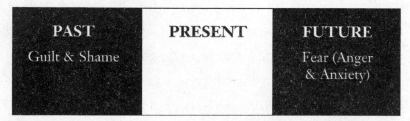

FIGURE 3.1. This diagram shows three constructs of time—the past, the present, and the future. Issues of guilt and shame that may lead to depression are about the past. Issues of fear are about the future and may present as anger and anxiety.

Guilt and Shame

Guilt is regret for some past action that was harmful to oneself or others. Often those who experience guilt feel some form of negative affect, especially depression, associated with the remembrance. (Fear, on the other hand, concerns the future, which is discussed below.)

Mild regret helps us make sense of life events and come up with remedies for what went wrong. It allows us to learn not only from our mistakes but also from the mistakes of others. Mild regret helps us recognize the difference between how things are and how they might have turned out if we had made a different choice.

On the other hand, excessive guilt is nothing more than a disguised form of narcissism. "See how terrible I am. God could never forgive me for what I have done," the narcissist says with head in hand and tears in his/her eyes. This just allows the ego to be exaggerated and blown up. It is like being the hero in your own tragic Greek play: "Oh, look at me." In this case, the error of the ego is inflated instead of relinquished to mild regret. The ego loves being the martyr.

Guilt can be nothing more than an attempt to buy salvation by manipulating God. We even try to purchase forgiveness by suffering. This comes from the misperception of God as a punitive instead of an all-loving and all-forgiving being.

As one's shortcomings come into the light, guilt and shame generally take middle stage. Shame is most often attuned to early-life developmental hurt. Such hurts include neglect and physical, sexual, and emotional abuse. Shame-based people sees themselves as broken or as inherently bad or flawed.

Shame says "I am bad," while guilt says "I did something bad." Guilt is related to unacceptable behavior and is a consequence of the memory of regretted past actions.

When someone says, "I am guilty," they are equating the actions of the former self with the current self. This is very important to realize, because to transcend guilt, we must change the context. For example, the thing you are most guilty about happened two years ago while you were extremely stressed out and in grave financial difficulty. Are you telling me that today you are exactly the same person you were then? Of course you aren't. How much more might you positively change if you stay on your spiritual path? This reframe allows us to see ourselves in the context of someone who is moving in a positive direction, as opposed to being stuck in the past.

Guilt is always about the past. Spending too much time in the past is an indulgence and does us little good. The energy, however, can be sublimated into positive change. As soon as you experience regret, ask for forgiveness. The feeling should pass. (Severe guilt, which is neurotic in nature, is paralyzing. It is an emotional judgment—not a factual one—about right or wrong. True conscience intervenes when a judgment is based on fact. Emotional judgment goes beyond "I did a wrong thing" by adding "and I am worthless.")

Feeling guilty is not bad. A person who has the capacity to feel guilt is in a much better place than someone who lacks the capacity for empathy. Being able to admit our errors shows we are progressively becoming more humble in nature. As a matter of fact, we probably did the best that we could under the circumstances. What you did may have also been important because what caused us guilt helped to escalate the pain level to such a degree that change was required, such as seeking professional help. The best treatment for guilt is to ask God for forgiveness; it is also good to ask forgiveness from the offended party unless doing so would cause further harm. It is also important to make a decision to change and never repeat the behaviors that caused the guilt.

Fear

In a spiritual sense, fear is an illusion that seems to be related to desire. Desire comes from a sense of personal "lack"—the feeling that something or someone is needed to make one feel whole. It is easy to see how harmful attachments to people or substances can stem from this internal "piece that is missing." The fear may be about not feeling good enough or feeling unworthy in some fashion. Sometimes, when nothing seems to allow relief from our fears, a sense of hopelessness arises.

Relative to the human condition, there are two primordial circumstances of living in the linear world that lie beneath our fears. The first of these conditions is the fear of alienation. To be banished from a group is, in many ways, akin to death. This comes from our evolutionary heritage, where to be banned from the tribe led to almost certain death. The second of these conditions is the fear of our mortality—the fear of death. Both of these fears are an illusion.

Nonlinear physics teaches us that we are all "one"— connected to everything in the universe through the energy of consciousness. Nonlinear physics calls the energy field that we are all connected to and a part of the zero-point field. I call the same energy field the Holy Spirit. This is the same energy field that overpowered me during my enlightenment experience. It is what Jesus called the "Comforter," and he sent it to his apostles when he departed this earth. There are many names for this field of energy. It is what existed prior to the "big bang" and from which all that we see, taste, smell, hear, and touch comes from. In the 1960s and '70s, we called it cosmic consciousness. It might also be called Divinity. The spiritual paths teach us that there is no death. The soul or Self has always been here and will always be here. Only the physical body, or shell, returns to its source: dust to dust.

Now that we have addressed the big fears in life, we can look at the little stuff of worldly fear. How can someone be realistically afraid of something that they have no way of knowing even exists? When you start to feel fearful, it is best to bring that feeling back into the moment and ask yourself, "If I am feeling fear about something that *might* happen, what can I do right now to strengthen myself so that I will be well equipped to handle what I fear?"

Fear carries a lot of energy. The energy itself is good and can be used to help you on your spiritual journey. However, "fear" is just a word that describes a multitude of symptoms, both physical and emotional. If I were to ask you, "What kind of physical symptoms do you experience when you are fearful?" and you answer, "My heart beats fast." I would reply, "If your heart beats fast, but not too fast, could you handle it?" Chances are, you could. Breaking down the fear into separate symptoms, such as a nervous stomach, perspiration, and so on, all of which can easily be tolerated separately, helps you to realize that you are bigger than your fears. These symptoms are more "manageable" when looked at this way than when you are overwhelmed by the nebulous and amorphous word "fear."

Fear may also be expressed as anger and anxiety. Anger and other external expressions of fear represent a need to control what feels unmanageable. It creates an interesting paradox— your fear and anger give people control over you. Think about this for a moment. When you allow people, places, and/or objects to cause you to respond with anxiety, fear, and anger, you have given that person or thing control over your reactions. No one I know would desire to hand over his/her control to someone or something else, and in fact, this is in opposition to what he/she is trying to get out of the situation: personal control.

Once we understand that we can never be alone because of the unity of everything in the universe, and that there is no death because the Self lives on forever, there is really no reason to fear anything. Once you lose the fear of fear, the world cannot control you anymore. At this point, you have internalized your energy and can spend more time in the moment where happiness and connection with God reside.

Fear is very much about projection into the future. The best way to let go of fear is to surrender it to God. The experiences of anger, fear, and anxiety cause an initial neurobiological response associated with the release of certain stimulatory neurotransmitters. Dr. Jill Bolte Taylor describes this experience:

> Once triggered, the chemical released by my brain surges through my body and I have a physiological response. Within 90 seconds from the initial trigger, the chemical component of my anger has completely dissipated from my blood and my automatic response is over. If, however, I remain angry after those 90 seconds have passed, then it is because I have chosen to let the circuit continue to run. Moment by moment, I make the choice to either hook into my neurocircuitry or move back into the present moment, allowing that reaction to melt away as fleeting physiology.[17]

This is my choice: to either stay in the egoic left hemisphere or move into the silence of the right hemisphere. The more spiritual energy one possesses, the easier it becomes to enter into the serenity of the right hemisphere. (For a better understanding of the right and left brain and the functions they play in the spiritual journey, see Chapter 9.)

---

[17] Jill Bolte Taylor, *My Stroke of Insight* (New York: Viking, 2006), 146.

If I choose to stay engaged with whatever made me angry, anxious, or fearful, interconnected loops of emotion and cognition start to take over. One loop is cognitive, and it says something like, "What a jerk. I don't know why he did that to me. I'll get even with Bob for that," and on and on this goes in repetitive loops, fueling the emotional loop to even greater heights. This can go on for hours, days, and even years. However, at the end of ninety seconds, I can calmly surrender, and in the moment say, "I surrender this anger that I have against Bob to you, God."

Remember that fear is an energy force behind the ego. Narcissism with its grandiose and prideful need to be better than others to cover our own immaturity leaves us emotionally sensitive to any real or perceived slight, and our response is often an angry overreaction. We simply had to look good to cover up our deep-seated inferiorities.

Hopelessness

Compared to fear, hopelessness presents itself as an extremely low level of spiritual energy, making even simple movement painful. Trying to negotiate the mountain would be extremely difficult, but the apathy of hopelessness precludes even effort. People who are feeling hopeless generally make little movement due to lack of energy and also to a negative belief that says, "Why should I try, for tomorrow will be just like today."

Hopelessness requires energy from the outside. It was at first hard for me to understand that just sitting with someone could be helpful to them. After sitting in silence with a wife who had just lost her husband, as I said my good-byes, she looked up at me and said, "Thank you." In my mind the talk was negative: *Why is she thanking me? I haven't done anything.* However, as you progress in your understanding of the spiritual world, you begin to understand this type of situation. To give of one's self using the energy of love is the greatest gift you can give to another human. It starts with the ability to see love and beauty inside of others when they cannot see it due to the conditions of their lives. When a person becomes more spiritually involved, the power of loving energy becomes apparent. It is healing.

Out of desire for something greater comes hope. We want to feel better about ourselves. Hope is gained from fellowship. We hear the stories of how others have traversed the valley of depression or the irregular landscape of anxiety and start to believe in our hearts that it can come true for us. The challenge is in how to reach out in hope. How do we know that our hopes are reasonable? We now know it can be done because it has been done. The "knowingness" of others who have been there and survived is very powerful. In listening, we also need to hear that they did not do it alone. Their ego did not get them back on track. We need to know that as one, I will fail, but as "ONE" with all of God's creation and darned good friends, *we*

will succeed. Never, ever underestimate the incredible, cura-
tive power of hope. The ego gets its juice from resentment and
anger. Those on the spiritual road get our "juice" from hope
and direction. Choose good teachers and be a good learner.

Of importance to us here is the concept of living in the
moment. One can only be happy while in the moment, and one
can only find God within the context of the moment.
Spirituality is all about being in the moment—nothing else
really exists.

The Importance Given to
Personal and Material Attachments

The Buddha taught that all suffering is due to either ignorance or attachment. Attachment can apply to many things. One
way of conceptualizing the problem of attachment is by asking
the question, "Am I giving so much importance to a person,
place, or thing that I lose sight of what is truly important—my
relationship with God?" Addiction is an attachment to a drug
such that the drug becomes so important that the addict will do
anything to maintain the relationship. A relationship becomes
an attachment when we lose sight of what we know to be
morally correct in order to maintain the relationship.

Codependency works in this way, as one person gives to
another beyond what they know is warranted. Work can
become an attachment when our mood is either positive or

negative depending upon the outcome. A good example of this is the work of a clinician. If clinicians allow the result of their work with the patient to determine their moods—feeling good when the patient does well and depressed if the patient relapses or does poorly—this is an unhealthy attachment. Whether we are parents, teachers, coaches, or clinicians, we should enter every relationship with love and integrity. It is up to the others to take our example, instruction, advice, and so on, and to use it for their betterment.

Jesus gives us many examples of how attachment to wealth or worldly things can get in the way of our truly discovering life. Jesus says, "He who desires to save his life shall lose it; and he who loses his life shall save it."[18] Jesus is referring to the loss of life as the loss of the ego. The ego is totally absorbed in worldly goods and acquisitions. Jesus further states, "How difficult it is for those who have wealth to enter into the kingdom of God! It is easier for a rope to go through the eye of a needle than for a rich man to enter the kingdom of God."[19]

The suffering caused by the functions of the ego creates incredible opportunities for spiritual growth. It seems that humility comes from humiliation. Life is, if nothing else, full of humiliation. Being kicked out of school for drug violations, I was put into jail and subsequently on parole. This led to incredible humiliation and self-doubt. It also led me to doubt the very God that I was bought up to believe in. If it was God

---

[18] Luke 17:33, *Holy Bible,* trans. George M. Lamsa.
[19] Luke 18:24–25, *Holy Bible,* trans. George M. Lamsa.

who caused all of this misery and pain in one's life, who really needed friends like Him? He didn't seem to be a very benevolent Higher Power. Of course, the ego blames every bad thing on something external and internalizes the good as personal virtue. I was a righteous addict who was being screwed by the system, and God wasn't doing a darn thing about it!

Obviously there was something wrong with the way I looked at the world. All of this was nothing more than a series of spiritual opportunities. Pride and righteous indignation just didn't allow me to see my life in that way. As I look at the world today, it seems that everyone on the news is trying to fight for the moral high ground. From here, righteous indignation seems to give permission to any type of egoic retaliation. Religion sometimes works in this way. It does seem utterly ridiculous to "Kill for Christ" or to destroy for "Allah the Most Merciful." Clearly, the spiritual journey is often very misunderstood.

*   *   *

In Chapter 4, I will endeavor to explain the meaning of some often-heard terms, such as *the consciousness field, spiritual transformation,* and *spirituality*. I will also introduce the three main pathways to spiritual transformation. Remember, there are many roads to God. Once we have looked more closely at the journey, we can devote our time to deflating the ego and allowing the Self to shine through. In the spiritual quest, as the ego's stranglehold is released, not only will the Self manifest, but you will notice the spiritual tool of humility growing stronger. All of this happens as the neurobiology of your brain starts to shift from left-hemisphere dominant to right-hemisphere dominant. The silence and serenity of the right hemisphere has many health and spiritual benefits.

4

Spiritual Transformation

Love not the world, neither the things that are in the world. He who loves the world, the love of the Father is not in him. For all that is in the world is the lust of the body, the covetousness of the eyes, and the pride of material things; these things do not come from the Father but from the world. And the world passes away, and the lust thereof; but he who does the will of God abides forever.[20]

---

[20] 1 John 2:15–17, *Holy Bible*, trans. George M. Lamsa.

As we wander through this world, we learn lessons about ourselves, others, and life in general. This allows us to see the world in a more mature way—what we call "growing up." However, when we really take a close look at what is growing within us, it is usually our egos. We are learning how to finesse the world, or at least that is what we think. Actually, the world of mass-media marketing, politics (tell them only what they can handle and lie about the rest), and various approaches such as New Age spirituality are finessing us. A secret message from God is not encoded in your DNA. There is no quick approach that for a few thousand dollars will skyrocket your spiritual self. All of this propaganda just gets us farther and farther away from the simple truth. If someone tells you that for five thousand dollars he/she will whisper the secret of the universe into your ear or he/she can make you an enlightened soul for several thousand, just walk away. These are all scams of the ego. What is freely received is freely given. What you already have cannot be purchased or acquired. It just is.

Remember that we are speaking of a subjective spiritual world. There are two different domains of human existence. One is the psychological domain that relates to our everyday life of thoughts, feelings, and behaviors. This domain is concerned with relative truths. In other words, what does a particular situation mean to me? For example, if my brother was killed overseas in a war against terrorism, it would impact me deeply as it has great personal meaning and involves an interpersonal relationship. We are speaking of the domain of form. Form is what we can see, feel, and relate to in our everyday functioning. This is the content of our everyday reality that involves our beliefs, thoughts, feelings, and memories. It is these aspects of this domain that lead to the formation of the ego's motives, opinions, and character flaws. This is the domain of human grief and suffering. This is the world that most people believe we are trapped in, with no way out but to die. This linear field of form is home to dualistic perspectives. It is the world of opposites. It is the world of blame. Fortunately, we can grow spiritually and understand that this world of form is only a tiny part of all that is: the infinite consciousness, or God.

This infinite domain of human consciousness is spiritual and subjective in nature. It involves the Absolute and absolute truth. This domain relates to what is infinite, timeless, and true eternally—for now and forever. It is beyond any individual viewpoint. From this view my brother's death is just another of many who passed away that day. There is a deeper understanding that there is no death; the soul has always been here and always will be here on its journey back to its source. This is the domain of context. Context is the unseen, infinite presence from which all content emerges. Context involves unconditional love, humility, and gratitude. It is the unmanifest from which the physical world of form emerges. For example, evolution and creation are not in any form of conflict.

Evolution is creation manifesting itself when the conditions are right. It is like the small seed in the ground when spring comes. With the rain and the sunshine, it sprouts, and if conditions continue to be right, it grows into a beautiful tree.

Nonduality reveals that at the core of all existence, everything and everybody is one, a single homogenous entity. In other words, if you "boil down" everything that exists, both perceived and unperceived, the result would be one single thing. From this single entity, everything manifest is derived. Without this entity, which I call the Holy Spirit (which you may call consciousness, the zero-point field, divinity, and so on), nothing whatsoever would exist.

All things exist simultaneously in the unmanifest universe, expressing itself in the manifest, or perception of form. These forms in reality have no independent existence but are the product of perception. (We experience these forms in our mind, but they do not independently exist outside of the mind.) Thoughts, emotions, and other mental phenomena appear to us to have an inherent personal quality. However, one ultimately finds that thoughts and mental pictures arise by themselves with no voluntary control from an independent self ("me"). Psychophysiological conditions come together to generate these mental pictures and thoughts, but there is no evidence that a separate self ("I") is among the causal influences.

This nonlinear field of context is the field of "Oneness" and spiritual connectedness. Achieving "Oneness" involves a congruent understanding of energy systems, as well as the heart. Neither is there a separate self nor any opposites. In nonduality there can be no opposites. Cold is not the opposite of hot; it is just the absence of heat. Dark is not the opposite of light; it is just the absence of light.

To reach a perpetual nonlinear state, one must get beyond the mind. In traditional Western society, the mind is everything, making any approach to getting beyond the mind counter to all of our teaching. The concept, often described in English as "nondualism," is extremely hard for the mind to grasp or visualize, since the mind constantly engages in the making of distinctions, and nondualism represents the rejection or transcendence of all distinctions.

Table 4.1. Linear and Nonlinear Reality	
Linear (Duality)	**Nonlinear (Nonduality)**
Objective	Subjective (Spiritual)
Newtonian Physics	Quantum Physics
Manifest World (Content)	Unmanifest World (Context)
Separate Self (Ego)	"Oneness"
Cause-Effect (Blame)	Effect
World of Opposites	Paradox of the Opposites

The understanding of linear and nonlinear reality is critical to the understanding of the subjective spiritual world. From the nonlinear world (unmanifest) comes the linear world (manifest). It is the manifest world that we can see, smell, touch, taste, and feel.

When we speak of the spiritual world, we talk about an entirely different way of looking at everything. In the world of form, we look to the physics of Sir Isaac Newton. There is always something that causes something else to happen. This is known as "cause-effect" determination and is often illustrated by a billiard ball hitting another billiard ball and causing a reaction. In the spiritual world, there is no cause, only effect. Everything happens of its own when conditions are right. We can look at the term "spiritual transformation" in this light. When one works a spiritual program with love and integrity, when conditions are right, the person grows spiritually. There is no "you" that wills or causes this to happen.

The spiritual world is considered subjective, while the linear world is considered objective. There is no such thing as true objectivity, as the laws of nonlinear physics describe. The linear world is a world of opposites where *if someone is not like me, there must be something wrong or bad about him/her.* This leads to blame and millions upon millions of deaths. In the nonlinear world, there are no opposites.

For most, the nonlinear world of the unmanifest (from which everything comes) seems mystical and even spooky. I want to demystify it for you by saying that all of you have been there many times. You may abide in the nonlinear realm, or you may be one of the vast majorities who are still working upward through the linear sphere. The nonlinear realm is outside of space and time. Have you ever lost track of time while watching a sunset or walking through nature? Have you ever spaced out or daydreamed and left the objective left brain? If you have done any or all of these things, you understand the nonlinear realm well. Think back to how that felt. Serene and peaceful.

Later we will look in detail at how the ego is deflated, what spiritual tools are utilized when working toward spiritual transformation, and how humility is such an important part of this process. We will see that what the ego often perceives as weakness—humility and surrender—turns out to be great strengths. For now, we will look at the often misunderstood concepts and phenomenon concerning consciousness, spiritual transformation, pathways to transformation, emergence of the Self, and the effect of conversion on the neurobiological system of the spiritual aspirant.

Please understand that the following is my own understanding based on the knowingness that I have received from my own spiritual transformation. All of us are on different legs of the journey toward spiritual transformation. I can only offer my experience with honesty, love, and integrity. There has been nothing done of my own; all has been a gift granted by God as I have prayed for Him to work through me.

What is spirituality?
What is a spiritual transformation?
What is spiritual consciousness?

What Is Spirituality?

In *Pathways to Spirituality*, Bill O'Hanlon speaks of spirituality in the following words: "When people seek therapy they are often feeling isolated, disconnected and disempowered, at least in some area of their lives. Spirituality, in this definition, begins with the opposite of this experience. It is a movement toward feeling connected to something bigger within or beyond oneself that can evoke feelings of competence or okayness."[21]

Just about everyone has some belief in a creative, life-giving force. We may think of this force as a Power rather than a person. This Power can be felt but not seen, very much like gravity. In the narrowest sense, "spirituality" refers to matters of the spirit. Spiritual matters concern the ultimate nature and meaning of humankind—our search and struggle for a higher meaning to this life.

Spirituality as a way of life concerns itself with aligning the human will and mind with that dimension of life and the subjective universe that is harmonious and ordered. As such, spiritual disciplines (which are often part of an established religious tradition or self-help group) enjoin practitioners (trainees or disciples) to cultivate those higher potentialities of the human being—such as wisdom, love, and gratitude—that are more concerned with matters other than the ego.

Spirituality involves the use of spiritual tools. These tools include but are not limited to love, humility, gratitude, appre-

---

[21] Bill O'Hanlon, *Pathways to Spirituality* (New York: W. W. Norton, 2006), 11–12.

ciation, forgiveness, and surrender. These tools are also inter-changeable, since practicing one (love, for example) will also involve kindness, forgiveness, and so on. These tools will become evident as we look at how to approach some of the difficult spiritual issues, such as fear, guilt, and grandiosity. Removing these illusions or "false ideas" allows for a closer connection to God. The spiritual quest is the quest for truth. For me, it does not involve "My will be done" but "Thy will be done." For others it may be "How can I serve?" As long as the quest is noble, it will lead to the same ultimate truth.

In this context, we are looking at spirituality as different from religion. Religion implies dogma, rituals, rules, and traditions that have been carried forth by the church. For me, the essence of who we are is the spiritual. The spiritual speaks to the core of what Jesus taught during his brief tenure on this earth. As Saint John stated, "For God is Spirit; and those who worship him must worship him in spirit and in truth."[22] Formalized religion has decided over time what one should believe and what one should do in order to become closer to God. My spiritual origins go back to the original translations of Jesus's teachings taken from the Aramaic of the Peshitta. Aramaic was the language that Jesus spoke. Remember, Christianity was born in the East.

There are many levels of spiritual attainment. A metaphor we may consider is that of climbing a mountain. Consider the

---

[22] John 4:24, *Holy Bible,* trans. George M. Lamsa.

level of one's spiritual understanding increasing as one strives to climb higher and higher. The vast majority of people live at the bottom of the mountain. Their lives are totally driven by ego and the drive to accumulate more in order to feel all right. This is a very lonely place because there is little loving connection to anything other than getting one's own needs met. These people live in the world of form and duality. Something or someone is always "causing" them to be angry, and they blame people, places, and things outside of themselves. This is why discrimination, prejudice, and war are so easy to sell. *Those people don't talk like we do, they don't believe in the things we do, and they don't look like us, so they must be wrong and therefore evil.* This is the material world, where if you cannot see it, it doesn't exist.

There are a sizable number who live in the foothills. They have developed higher moral standards and an increased spiritual sense. They strive to treat others well and live lives of compassion. There is the realization of something out there greater than them, and they probably are on the path to climb even farther up the mountainside. The notion of God and how God works in their lives exists as part of their perspective. Moral standards are important determinants of behavior, and the commandment "treat your neighbor as thyself" reveals concern and true caring for others.

As we ascend the mountain, we find fewer and fewer people, and the path is not well traveled. At this level, life is known to be sacred. These individuals have entered the nonlinear aspects of being. There is an understanding that love is not a feeling but comes from the heart and is a way of being in the world. There is the realization that everything is truly One. At this level, everything in life truly starts to work out. You are now congruent with consciousness, or on the same wavelength, so to speak. At this level, those who have intimately worked a spiritually based program are capable of the experience of unconditional love or an experience of total serenity. They see life and its inhabitants as being just the way they are supposed to be in the perfection of God's creation. There is true joy at this level, as one can now appreciate that true happiness comes from selfless service. It is what you give to the world, not what the world gives to you that is important. The "taker" has become a "giver."

Those who have climbed the mountain are very rare. Often those who have climbed this far have permission to leave this world, for they have mastered this life. The ones who remain may live a quiet life, drawing no attention to themselves, or they may become teachers and mentors to others who are aspiring to live the spiritual life. There is no real end of the path or top of the mountain for them, as there is an endless need for personal growth and service to others. The terms utilized to describe this most rare of individuals are enlightened (as in returning to the Light), union with God, and *unio mystica* (mystical union). Each spiritual discipline has its own words to describe this experience. Here one lives his/her life like a prayer, understanding that goodness, prayer, and acts of kindness elevate everyone. There is no "you," "us," or "them"; we are all One. To give and to receive are synonymous—an outstretched hand to the world.

Radical, transformative, spiritual consciousness (enlightenment) is rare. Ken Wilber, hailed as one of today's brightest and most original spiritual thinkers, says:

> *First, although it is generally true that the East has produced a greater number of authentic realizers, nonetheless, the actual percentage of the Eastern population that is engaged in authentic transformative spirituality is, and has always been, pitifully small. I once asked Katgiri Roshi, with whom I had my first breakthrough (hopefully not a breakdown), how many truly great Ch'an and Zen masters there have historically been. Without hesitating, he said, "Maybe one thousand altogether." I asked another Zen master how many truly enlightened—deeply enlightened—Japanese Zen masters there were alive today, and he said, "Not more than a dozen."*
>
> *Let us simply assume, for the sake of argument, that those are vaguely accurate answers. Run the numbers. Even if we say there were only one billion Chinese over the course of its history (an extremely low estimate), that still means that only one thousand out of one billion had graduated into an authentic, transformative spirituality. For those of you without a calculator, that's 0.0000001 of the total population.*

The numbers quoted by Dr. David Hawkins, one of the world's leading teachers on the path to enlightenment, are as small as those given by Wilber. Using the science of kinesiology, Dr. Hawkins states that the number of fully enlightened people residing on this earth today is six. This number was given in his 2006 book *Transcending the Levels of Consciousness*.[23]

In summary, spirituality is a unique and intense experience of a reality greater that oneself or an experience with the "oneness" of all things. Religion is organized around rules, dogma, and stories within which spiritual experiences can be shared and passed on to subsequent generations of worshippers. However, one does not have to subscribe to any particular religious belief to be spiritually inclined. Being an individual who seeks a spiritual path leads one either slowly or quickly to discover strengths that may have been hidden in the past. These benefits include:

- Humility
- Inner Strength
- Sense of meaning and purpose in life
- Forgiveness
- Gratitude
- Acceptance
- Harmony and serenity
- True happiness

---

[23] David Hawkins, *Transcending the Levels of Consciousness* (West Sedona, AZ: Veritas, 2006), 275.

What Is Spiritual Transformation?

The spiritual journey can be very lonely and painful, but the rewards of spiritual transformation are more than worth the trip. According to Father Thomas Keating, "This predicament is identified by a need for escape from the circle of ever-recurring evil habits with their ensuing misery. The Christian tradition regards the cure of this malaise as a return to intimacy with God, which is the source of human wholeness."[24]

When the spiritual journey is embarked upon, wholeness—freedom from attachments—is the reward. Spiritual transformation begins when one recognizes that he/she has a need to escape, or as Mel Ash writes in *The Zen of Recovery*:

> *At the moment of true ego deflation, our deep attachments to our thoughts, our disease and its progression fly away like dry leaves in a mighty dharma. We stand naked, stripped of even the last remnant of personal identity. The yoke of our disease has been broken. The lifelong enslavement to desire, addiction and self-destruction has simply vanished. It isn't done logically. It isn't done rationally. It's done by a great intuitive leap ignited by our sheer and utter desperation. We are like a pot of water brought to a boiling point by the immensity of our suffering and by our sudden recognition that we ourselves are the source of our disease and suffering, and that we are the means to ending it.* [25]

---

[24] Thomas Keating, *The Heart of the World* (New York: Crossroad, 1981), 40.
[25] Mel Ash, *The Zen of Recovery* (New York: Jeremy P. Tarcher/Putnam, 1993), 97.

Out of our desperation comes our redemption, as well as our destiny. For an illustration of this, let's look at the relationship between Carl Jung and Roland Hazard, as reported by Bill Wilson in his 1969 U.S. Senate testimony:

> I refer to Carl Jung, who in the early 1930s received a patient from America, a well-known businessman. He had run the gamut of the cures of the time and desperately wanted to stop and could get no help at all. He came to Jung and stayed with him about a year. He came to love the great man. During this period the hidden springs of his motivation were revealed. He felt now with this new understanding, plus communication with this new and wonderful friend, that he had really shed this strange illness of mind, body and spirit.
>
> Leaving there, he was taken drunk, as we AA's say, in a matter of a month, perhaps, and coming back, he said, "Carl, what does this all mean?" Then this man made a statement which I think led to the formation of AA. It took a great man to make it. He said, "Roland, up until recently I thought you might be one of those rare cases who could be aided and made to recover by the practice of my art. But like most who will pass through here, I must confess that my art can do nothing for you." "What?" said the patient. "Doctor, you are my port of last resort. Where will I turn now? Is there no other recourse?" The doctor said, "Yes, there may be. There is the off-chance. I am speaking to you of the possibility of a spiritual awakening, if you like, a conversion." "Oh," said the patient. "but I am a religious man. I used to be a vestryman in the Episcopal Church. I still have faith in God, but He has little in me, I should think." Jung said, "I mean something that goes deeper

than that, Roland, not just a question of faith."

Dr. Jung continued, "I am talking about a transformation of spirit that can motivate you and set you free from this. Time after time alcoholics have recovered by these means. The lightning strikes here and there and no one can say why or how. All I can suggest is that you expose yourself to some religious environment of your own choice." [26]

Looking back at the mountain, we can see Roland somewhere near the bottom, struggling in an egoic fashion to climb to the top. The psyche, which is the haven of the ego, can never facilitate a spiritual transformation through an examination of itself. Remember, we are not talking about a matter of the intellect but of the heart. At this juncture, absolute surrender to God is the greatest of practices. We are saying to God, "Take me, do with me as you will. I put myself in Your hands now because on my own I cannot make it. My ego is clever and has a lot of schemes, but they are all doomed to fail." Psychology deals with the human psyche, which contains the ego. Spirituality deals with something far greater than the individual self.

Unfortunately, few humans are willing to come to grips with the enormity of the task of surrender. To view the large gap between the way one imagines himself/herself to be and the

---

[26] Bill Wilson's 1969 U.S. Senate Testimony before the Special Subcommittee on Alcoholism and Narcotics of the Committee on Labor and Public Welfare, United States Senate, Ninety-first Congress, First Session, on Examination of the Impact of Alcoholism, Thursday, July 24, 1969. Accessed online at http://www.rewritables.net/cybriety/bill w%27s_testimony.htm.

way he/she really is truly a painful and humbling experience. This path can lead to a sudden or gradual unwillingness to compromise what it means to fully be a human being. Some people may never embark upon the spiritual journey, and many who do may never experience spiritual transformation. Perhaps this is because they are trapped in their own intellectual being and cannot attain the "oneness" necessary for understanding the nonlinear realm of consciousness. Or it may be due to personality extremes that trap them in antisocial behavior and severe grandiosity, never allowing them to see beyond themselves. Here we are interested in the other two types of individuals—those who have had rapid spiritual conversions and those whose conversions happen after years of struggle along the path. The latter type is the most common. One experience seems to be no better or more enduringly profound than the other.

Nonlinear physics introduces us to the Law of Sensitive Dependence on Initial Conditions. This law assists in our understanding of the type of radical conversion taking place over some period of time. Although there appears to be no discrete time frame to this process, we might think it would take months to many years of searching for the truth. Here we find that, in the beginning, a small variation in a pattern of inputs (in this case information put into your mind) can result in a very large change in eventual outputs.

When we change our thought patterns and the resulting

habitual responses over time through persistence, dedication, and repetition, larger changes can occur down the line. For example, by staying straight one day at a time, Martha B.— over a period of approximately five years—went from a desperate state of chronic alcoholism to the serene state of total acceptance of life and its resulting serenity. Her health, marriage, and career were all restored and strengthened. She is also the sponsor of two other women. One has recently completed three years of uninterrupted sobriety. Martha and many like her were able, through complete honesty and humility, to open themselves up. The crack in the overwhelmed ego led to a chance for the light to shine through and for the Holy Spirit to do its work.

My personal spiritual journey toward enlightenment took place over many years of study and preparation and culminated in the experience I discussed in Chapter 1. And there are other very similar stories. One of my favorites is the narrative of Elisabeth Kübler-Ross. While in the throes of severe pain, she describes the end of the ego as labor pains:

It became, for the first time in my life, an issue of faith. And the faith had something to do with a deep inner knowledge that I had the strength and the courage to endure this agony by myself. But it also included the faith and the knowledge that we are never given more than we can bear. I suddenly became aware that all I needed to do was to stop my fight, to stop my rebellion, to stop being a warrior and move from rebellion to a simple, peaceful, positive submission to the ability to simply say "yes" to it.

Once I did that, the agony stopped and my breathing was easier. My physical pain disappeared at the moment I uttered the word "yes," not in words but in thoughts. And instead of the thousand deaths, I lived through a rebirth beyond human description . . . [She goes on to describe the experience of the pulsating light that replaced everything that her eyes could see. When merging into the light, she states,] I became one with it. [27]

In other cases, there is a very rapid, spontaneous transformation of consciousness, such as that experienced by Bill Wilson. Although he said he did not believe in God and believed only in the power of his own ego, Bill Wilson found himself crying out, "If there be a God, let him show himself!" The response he reported was amazing. "Suddenly my room blazed with an indescribably white light. I was seized with an ecstasy beyond all description. Every joy I had known was pale by comparison." He later wrote, "Then seen in the mind's eye, there was a mountain. I stood upon its summit where a great wind blew. A wind, not of air but of spirit. In great, clean strength it blew right through me. Then came the blazing thought, 'you are a free man.'"[28] Bill understood this experience in the context of "So this is the God of the preachers."[29]

The process of spiritual transformation involves the deflation of the ego, either in a sudden fashion or over a longer period of time, and the growth of honesty to self, others, and

---

[27] Kubler-Ross, *On Life After Death*, 66–67.
[28] Susan Cheever, *My Name Is Bill* (New York: Washington Square Press, 2004), 118.
[29] Ibid., 121.

one's God. There is a sudden or steady movement up the mountain. The higher one gets on that mountain, the more the view differs. It is not that the mountain or the world surrounding the mountain has changed; it is the individual's perspective that is drastically different. Instead of seeing everything through the glasses of the ego, the Self is shining through. The Self is about love, appreciation, acceptance, understanding, and gratitude. The Self accepts others for who they are, without any desire to control or change any individual or situation, for the Self knows that you cannot change other people, as they will not change to be what another thinks they should be (think of all the human misery this type of struggle has wrought).

Spiritual transformation involves movement up the mountain. It does not define how far up the mountain one climbs. That is personal and by God's grace. In experiences where the seeker crosses over into the nonlinear realm, the state may not be steady. For example, near-death experiences (NDE) often describe elements of the enlightenment experience. However, after an NDE, the individual may end up higher in their level of spiritual consciousness but not necessarily reside in a nonlinear realm.

While conducting a course on advanced spiritual teachings, I mentioned near-death experiences where people had experienced the "light" and had been met by friends, but returned to this world because there was some unfinished business remaining. One of my students, Christine, came to me during the lunch break and told me the following story. "I tried to kill myself by drinking alcohol and taking some sleeping pills. I couldn't see any reason to live, and living was so miserable and seemed so hopeless." She went on to say that sometime later she awoke to see her five-year-old son standing beside the couch she was lying on. He had tears in his eyes. "This moment was so powerful," she said. "I immediately devoted my life to my son. I have been sober and straight for seven years now, and I am trying to be the best mother I can possibly be. Up until this point I believed if I told people of this experience, they would think I was crazy. I never understood what happened until now."

Experiences like these are life altering. Christine's intention in life was dramatically changed. She raised all of us up as she elevated herself. These types of experiences seem to greatly alter the individual and change their perception of the world. The people I have spoken with who have had such experiences generally have lost the fear of death. Death is a dualistic linear concern, perceived as the opposite of life.

Another interesting aspect of spiritual transformation is its effective duration. There have been situations when after swift or slower spiritual ascension, the individuals slide back down the mountain. At this point, some utilize the experience to climb even higher up the mountain. This might be perceived as a spiritual opportunity hidden within a spiritual opportunity. As mentioned, there really is no top of the mountain—no point when one can say, "I have helped others enough," "I know everything there is to know," or "I have arrived."

In order to successfully embark on a journey of spiritual transformation, the following should be helpful: First, appreciate and accept totally—not just in the mind but with the heart—that there is an energy field or some sort of organizing principle (consciousness) operating behind linear reality. In making this appreciation, one enters into the nonlinear world, which is formless and governed by intuitive knowing or "knowingness." As a child, you were encouraged to find your unique separateness. Now, reverse this trend so that boundaries between self and experience can be relaxed, much like the integrated, nonlinear experience of a young child.

What Is Spiritual Consciousness?

We join spokes together in a wheel,
but it is the center hole
that makes the wagon move.

We shape clay into a pot,
but it is the emptiness inside
that holds whatever we want.

We hammer wood for a house,
but it is the inner space
that makes it livable.

We work with being,
but non-being is what we use.[30]

These words were taken from the eleventh chapter of the *Tao Te Ching* written by Lao-tzu. The simple poetic beauty of the words yields a concept that is often very difficult for the spiritual seeker to grasp. The context is more important than the content when it comes to understanding the spiritual world. What is behind, all around, invisible, and the essence from which all is created is unseen to the human eye and unheard by the human ear. As the Tao relates, it is the spokes that join the wheel together, but without the space at the hub, it would not be very functional. It is the space inside of the pot that gives it utility. This is the nonlinear realm of being.

Another example of seeing things from a different perspective comes from an old Bible saying that goes, "We read the Bible day and night. You read black, while I read white." Like the message of Jesus, the truth is often found between the lines and not in the literal meaning of the words.

Consciousness is an infinite energy field where *everything* is stored. (Every hair is accounted for, and no sparrow is lost.) It

---

[30] Lao-tzu, the *Tao Te Ching*, Chapter 11. Found online at http://academic. brooklyn.cuny.edu/core9/phalsall/texts/taote-v3.html.

includes the physical world (manifest) and the nonmaterial world (the nonmanifest). Consciousness can be compared to the ever-expanding information field we call the Internet or the World Wide Web, in that it is a vast storage house of information. However, unlike the Internet, where it is sometimes difficult to distinguish truth from falsehood, the consciousness field contains only the truth. Consciousness contains the linear field of cause and effect—the world of classical Newtonian physics—although the greatest part of the consciousness field is the nonlinear, where there is no cause, only effect, occurring when conditions are suitable. There are many names given to the field of consciousness, such as the zero-point field (from nonlinear physics), the Holy Spirit, cosmic consciousness, and others.

Let's go back to the beginning of life as described in the biblical story. Everyone is at least somewhat familiar with the story of Adam and Eve from the book of Genesis. In Genesis 2:7 the story goes, "And the Lord God formed Adam out of the soil of the earth, and breathed into his nostrils the breath of life; and man became a living being."[31] God gave us the breath of life, the Light, or the Holy Spirit working within us. We can also call this the Self, God immanent, or the soul.

From their home with God in the nonlinear realm of being, we can only imagine what Adam and Eve's life was like. Obviously, the word "nonlinear" comes to mind, but I also

---

[31] Genesis 2:7, *Holy Bible,* trans. George M. Lamsa.

think of uncomplicated, natural, orderly, innocent, awestruck, childlike, non-egoic, and peaceful. In Genesis 2:9, we read, "And out of the ground the Lord God made to grow every tree that is pleasant to the sight and good for food; the tree of life also in the midst of the garden, and the tree of knowledge of good and evil." Reading further, in Genesis 2:16–17, "And the Lord God commanded the man, saying, 'Of every tree of the garden you may freely eat; But of the tree of the knowledge of good and evil, you shall not eat; for in that day that you eat of it you will surely die.'"[32] As the story goes, the serpent's temptation hooked the naïveté of Adam and Eve, and they ate of the forbidden fruit. Their death amounted to being banished from the nonlinear realm into the limited and linear realm of duality. For good and evil was the first duality. In the garden there was originally only "oneness" with all things being connected. There were no opposites. Evil was not the opposite of good. There was only good with evil symbolizing the absence but not the opposite of good.

Continuing the story in Genesis, "Then the eyes of both of them were opened, and they knew that they were naked; and they sewed fig leaves together, and made themselves aprons."[33] When Adam and Eve heard the voice of the Lord God calling for them in the garden, they hid themselves among

---

[32] Genesis 2:9 and 2:16–17, *Holy Bible*, trans. George M. Lamsa.
[33] Genesis 3:7, *Holy Bible*, trans. George M. Lamsa.

the trees in the garden. God said, "Where are you Adam?"[34] And ever since this time, humankind has been playing the primordial game of hide-and-seek, hiding not only our physical parts but also and more so our psychological parts, both from ourselves and others. We also live in the world of duality— little ball hits big ball and makes it move. This world of duality is the realm of the ego and the source of all the suffering in the world today. Instead of oneness and the ability to see the love and beauty inside another human being, we look for differences and strive for the moral high ground as we cast dispersions on anyone and everyone who doesn't look like, act like, or think like we do. This gives us a great many people to blame and reasons to justify all prejudice and negative action against our fellowman. This creates a world full of anger and hatred.

Let's continue to use the mountain as a source of reference and also imagine that this mountain is 10,000 feet high. At the lower levels of spiritual consciousness, the world is viewed from an egoic perspective. The person is very self-centered and grandiose, locked in behavioral patterns of self-service. This is generally where most of humankind resides, abiding by the rules of the "taker." This role is the reason for great suffering because it is not the acquisitions that make us happy; it is the total emptying of ourselves in selfless service that leads to a true state of contentment and serenity. The contemplative Christian term that approximates this on a very high level is "kenosis." It

---

[34] Genesis 3:9, *Holy Bible*, trans. George M. Lamsa.

speaks of the Father and the Son totally emptying themselves, one into the other, in a perpetual state of giving and receiving. As we empty ourselves, we allow the Holy Spirit to fill us. As we start to let go of our sense of difference and start to notice that we are like the others in the room, we begin to lose our fear of alienation and find comfort in fellowship. Hearing ourselves in others creates a sense of universality—I am not alone. Universality creates a sense of hope. Hope gives us more energy and starts to nudge us up the mountain. Never underestimate the power of hope. From hope springs forth dreams of things far greater than the reality of the present moment.

Courage gives us more energy and another push up the mountain. We start to understand that we really know little or nothing about anything, and we are not as smart as we used to think. We discover that our greatest thinking created an incredible amount of misery and suffering for ourselves and others in our lives. It is interesting how we live the fallacy of thinking that our egos have the answers to the problems it has created over and over again. I believe this is an apt definition of insanity.

We move higher up the mountain as we discover truth and humble ourselves by admitting our wrongs, asking God to remove our character defects, and becoming totally willing to make amends to those we have hurt. As you can see, this appears to be a very painful process. However, if performed with integrity and honesty, it can be a joyful reunion. At this point on the mountainside, a person has gained integrity and greater degrees of honesty. Some never go beyond this point, but still, this is a tremendous leap of consciousness considering where they started. This is an area of great reason and understanding. This transformation from seeing the world from a totally egoic perspective to understanding our inter-subjective relationships to others and dealing with life with greater integrity and honesty comes from the discovery of more of our true Self along with partial depletion of the ego.

There is a crucial point about halfway up the mountain. At this juncture, one moves from the linear dimension into the nonlinear one. For so many of us who are dependent on our left hemisphere reasoning and ability to intellectually understand things, this is a very large hurdle. This is the realm of love at the low end and supreme Love as one gathers more spiritual energy. At the low end is conditional love, where the higher spiritual consciousness deals with unconditional love.

From the scientific perspective, nonlinear physics and neurobiology has led us toward the understanding that everything is connected, everything is energy, and is everything is one. From the spiritual perspective, this is where the journey moves from the mind into the heart. At this loftier level, the spiritual seeker's journey strains to deal with strong links of duality (I-you, us-them). For example, one of the conundrums I dealt with early on in my spiritual journey was, "How can I love someone who blows up a busload of children?" I could intellectually understand that God was inside of that person as He is inside of me. Jesus said that if you are angry at your brother (another human) you are, in essence, angry at him, for we all received our life energy from the same source. On its own, my mind could never come to any sort of equilibrium with this, as at the end of the day, my ego still said, "Kill the SOB."

After digesting this controversy for nearly a month, the answer came to me. It was an answer without words. While walking in the yard, with my mind drifting, I felt a movement in my chest, and the dilemma was resolved. This is somewhat like an "aha" moment, but one of great depth, as now my whole being was in synchrony with the idea of loving. Unconditional love is a way of being in the world that moves one beyond the intellect and into the nonlinear understanding that things are happening on their own as conditions dictate. Love is not dependent on someone or something outside of you. One chooses to be Love in each moment as the moment unfolds, regardless of what happened in that moment. Everything is God's creation. If I stand in judgment of any person or situation, am I not playing God? The Lord said, "Judgment is mine." Unconditional love is a deep level of acceptance that allows people to see the love and beauty in all things that exist, even if they cannot see them in themselves. It is also important to understand that you can unconditionally love others and not agree with what their actions are. That is the case here. I do not agree with any act of violence or transgression against the life or rights of another. However, it is

God's job to make judgment and not mine.

The experience of unconditional love is a wonderful thing to strive for in this lifetime. It is a very serene place and is where a great "joy in living" is experienced. I have noticed how others gravitate toward people who exude unconditional love. There is something quite gentle about them. Yet, at the same time, they are honest and forthright in sharing their "knowingness." They have a calm and approachable demeanor and are very willing to be of service.

It is always important to remember that no energy level or perch on the mountain is any better than any other. Each person is perfectly where he/she is on the journey back home. We all are right where we are in order to learn the lessons that life has placed before us. It is wonderful to be a human being where, at every moment in time based on our understanding of what God expects from us, we get the opportunity to choose.

In summary, spiritual transformation can involve a small or a great leap in one's level of spiritual consciousness. All spiritual movement takes us closer to the truth and closer to our Self. There are many paths and spiritual tools that can help you on your journey. The next chapter describes the three historical paths to spirituality—the path of the heart, the path of the mind, and the path of action. Within each path are multitudes of pathways. Everybody's journey is different.

5

The Three Paths to Spiritual Transformation

All of us dwell on the brink of the infinite ocean of life's creative power. We carry it within us: supreme strength, the fullness of wisdom, unquenchable joy. It is never thwarted and cannot be destroyed. But it is hidden deep, which is what makes life a problem. The infinite is down in the darkest, profoundest vault of our being, in the forgotten well-house, the deep cistern. What if we could bring it to light and draw from it unceasingly? [35]

—Huston Smith

[35] Huston Smith, *The World's Religions,* (New York: HarperCollins, 1991), 26.

Throughout the ages, the world's great spiritual movements have focused on the development of techniques to ascend to higher levels of consciousness. Consequently, there are many paths you can take to move forward spiritually. No matter the path you choose, a radical and unwavering commitment to yourself and to God to be more accepting, forgiving, loving, understanding, and kinder is required.

The work of Dr. Andrew Newberg, director of the Center for Spirituality at the University of Pennsylvania, has shown that spiritual practices enhance the neural firing of certain areas of the brain. This enhancement in neural transmission can improve both physical and emotional health. Dr. Newberg's brain-imaging studies reveal that a specific circuit (which involves the prefrontal cortex, orbitofrontal cortex, anterior cingulate gyrus, basal ganglia, and thalamus) has an important role in clarity of mind, consciousness, empathy, emotional balance, and compassion. This same circuit suppresses fear and anger. If this circuit deteriorates or malfunctions, it contributes to mental-health problems such as depression and anxiety. Engaging in spiritual applications and exercises, including meditation and contemplation, cannot only keep this circuit healthy but strengthen the circuit itself.[36]

Surrounding ourselves with beauty, such as a breathtaking piece of art, a majestic mountain, or sweet music, allows for more time in the right hemisphere and can create awe-inspir-

---

[36] Andrew Newberg, *How God Changes Your Brain* (New York: Ballentine Books, 2009) 28–29.

ing (numinosum) experiences that can also positively impact our neurobiology (see Chapter 9 for more on this).

Last year, my son and I were at the Metropolitan Museum of Art in New York City. I was totally absorbed in the beauty of Raphael's work and could have sat there seemingly forever. It was an experience outside of time. Feeling a tap on my shoulder, I turned to see my seventeen-year-old son with a frown on his face. "Dad, this is really boring," he said. Needless to say, no avenue is for everyone, and timing is critical as to what works for you on your own personal journey. My son was not sharing my experience.

About five years ago, I began listening to classical music. As a former rock and roller, this was a new interest. I found that the beauty of classical music—though I don't profess to have a great understanding of the times, the composers, or the different instruments—moved me into that place where there is no time (in other words, being in the moment). Native American drum and flute, as well as jazz, can do similar things for me. Beauty isn't only relegated to art and music, of course. There is much beauty in any given moment if you stop to see and listen. Because of the incredible stimulation of this modern world we live in, some people have difficulty being in the moment. In that case, a walk in nature away from the hustle and bustle or meditation in a quiet place can help.

In his book *Transcending Levels of Consciousness,* Dr. David Hawkins speaks of simple tools of great value that have bought impressive results for spiritual aspirants over the centuries. He lists the following:

> *Be kind to everything and everyone, including oneself, all the time, with no exception.*
>
> *Revere all of life in all its expressions, no matter what, even if one does not understand it.*
>
> *Presume no actual reliable knowledge of anything at all. Ask God to reveal its meaning.*
>
> *Intend to see the hidden beauty of all that exists—it then reveals itself.*
>
> *Forgive everything that is witnessed and experienced, no matter what. Remember Christ, Buddha, and Krishna said that all error is due to ignorance. Socrates said all men choose only what they believe to be the good.*
>
> *Approach all of life with humility and be willing to surrender all positionalities and mental/emotional arguments or gain.*
>
> *Be willing to forego all perceptions of gain, desire, or profit and thereby be willing to be of selfless service to life in all of its expressions. Make one's life a living prayer by intention, alignment, humility, and surrender. True spiritual reality is actually a way of being in the world.*[37]

One of the best ways to tell if your spiritual path is working is to notice the change in energy flow. Where at one time you were struggling to supply the energy to move forward in your spiritual work and readings, now it is as if you are being pulled

---

[37] Hawkins, *Transcending the Levels of Consciouness*, 333–34.

from the future. It becomes effortless. You look forward to the quiet times alone or with others of a like mind-set and the reflective meditations concerning your life. There is an enhanced, joyful energy, making your spiritual program more simply and profoundly gratifying. You are on the road to a profound spiritual transformation.

There seems to be a relationship between total surrender and acceptance of life as being exactly the way God planned for it to be and this pull into the future. We actually realize that God doesn't need our help. Everything is the way it is on purpose, and although we don't understand it most of the time, we have become comfortable in its presence. Grace has been established within the mystery.

This may be a good time to clear up the issue of religion and spirituality in as far as our search for spiritual growth is concerned. Having been raised in a Christian home, I place great value on the religion of my youth. However, in the depths of my problems, I never felt the church, in itself, could save me. For some, it is a place of sanctuary. When I looked for answers, I went as far back to the original teachings of Jesus available to me. The New Testament is filled with the spiritual teachings of Jesus. He was considered a revolutionary and a counterculture troublemaker who reserved his most scathing criticism for those who were considered the most religious during his earthly lifetime (the Pharisees, whom he called "whitewashed tombs" because they followed all of the outer religious rules, but were actually dead inside). The dogma of the church left me cold, but the words of Jesus—especially if looked at through nonlinear glasses—were exciting. For example, the Beatitudes are Jesus's path to spiritual transformation. A very beautiful path to enlightenment resides in these eight blessed statements found in the Sermon on the Mount:

The Eight Beatitudes of Jesus

Blessed are the poor in spirit, for theirs is the kingdom of heaven.

Blessed are they who mourn, for they shall be comforted.

Blessed are the meek, for they shall inherit the earth.

Blessed are they who hunger and thirst for righteousness, for they shall be satisfied.

Blessed are the merciful, for they shall obtain mercy.

Blessed are the pure of heart, for they shall see God.

Blessed are the peacemakers, for they shall be called children of God.

Blessed are they who are persecuted for the sake of righteousness, for theirs is the kingdom of heaven.

Matthew 5:3–10 (Lamsa edition)

To quote the words of Ken Wilber, who takes a rather harsh but honest look at the role of the church in the spiritual journey:

I have tried to show that religion itself has always per-formed two very important, but different, functions. One, it acts as a way of creating meaning for the separate self (author-ego): it offers myths and stories and tales and narra-tives and rituals and revivals that, taken together, help the separate self make sense of, and endure, the slings and arrows of outrageous fortune. This function of religion does not usually or necessarily change the level of consciousness in a person; it does not deliver radical transformation. Nor does it deliver a shattering liberation from the separate self altogether. Rather, it consoles the self, fortifies the self, defends the self, and promotes the self. As long as the separate self believes the myths, performs the rituals, mouths the prayers, or embraces the dogma, then the self, it is fervently believed, will be "saved"—either now in the glory of being God-saved or Goddess-favored, or in an afterlife that ensures eternal wonderment.

He goes on to say, "But two, religion has also served—in a very, very, very small minority—the function of radical transformation and liberation. This function of religion does not fortify the separate self, but utterly shatters it . . . "[38] I believe Wilber is talking about the spiritual transformation that some seek within the structure of a religion. For most it is not transformative but allows one to understand and endure their world, which seems unfair and chaotic. Both functions are important. It just depends on what one is looking for. For the true spiritual seeker, religion can serve as a platform for deeper investigation. What is the deeper nonlinear meaning?

Quite often when spiritual seekers adhere to the inventive words of a prophet who started a spiritual movement, the path

---

[38] http://www.enlightennext.org/magazine/j12/wilber.asp?ifr=hp-edt.

is clear as is without human alteration or interpretation. It is the path that leads to spiritual freedom. Religion has been, and still is, the most important cohesive factor that any culture has. It is unfortunate, however, that humans claiming God's authority have decided what others should read, hear, and understand about the original teachings.

The book of Matthew 5:3–11 reveals a spiritual path that seems to encourage setting your sights on something more fulfilling and enduring than the frivolous material world. Don't let other people determine your worth based on super-ficial ideas. Find out what you believe to be true and stand for that with integrity and honesty. Don't let others set your value systems for you. Other people's approval is not what is required for eternal life. What matters is in the eyes and heart of God where ugly is beautiful, unpopular is "in," and abstain-ing from desires is satisfaction. The Beatitudes start with becoming humble, as the kingdom of heaven belongs to those with humility.

Jesus questioned and challenged the conventional wisdom and status quo of his time. He said that you must act from a heart of unconditional love and not from what society and family and friends tell you is right. There are continuous refer-ences in the New Testament to losing your life by trying to save yourself. Jesus is saying that we must get rid of our egos in order to find the Self. Human life is a path, and one must be open to the path. Jesus never said, "Blessed are you with a large 401K plan, for you will live comfortably throughout all your days." The message is always to set your sights on something more enduring and more fulfilling. Make your deposits in heaven and accumulate your riches in the kingdom, because everything on Earth disappears.

Now let's try to pull this litany of thoughts into the simplest understanding of the paths to spiritual transcendence. Remember that spirituality as a philosophy has a history of five thousand years or more. The great philosophers of Greece such as Aristotle and Plato were spiritual thinkers. Looking at this long and vast history brings us into contact with various claims regarding the search for enlightenment. Unfortunately, many charlatans have given this history a bad name. The ego will try to profit from anyone's misery. The truth is we are spiritual beings on our journey back home, and there are tried and true methods that help us move into levels of higher and higher spiritual energies. The three traditional paths are:

The Path of the Heart
The Path of the Mind
The Path of Action

Each of these paths is aided by prayer, meditation, and contemplation. All pathways seek to allow the seeker to let go of attachments and aversions, accept everything just the way it is, and focus on the perfection of all creation in a nonjudgmental way. There are characteristics of the adherent that

increase the probability of spiritual transformation. Remember, however, that any spiritual conversion is a gift from
God and occurs when conditions are attuned. The adherent
does his/her part by:

1. Being *focused* on the task
2. Being *committed* to his/her intention
3. Being *devoted* to the spiritual work
4. Being *forgiving* of self and others
5. Being *loving* of self and others
6. Being *nonjudgmental*
7. Being *understanding* of self and others
8. Being *silent* and being *still*

Hinduism built its spiritual paths on the basic personality type
of the individual aspirant (Carl Jung built his typology on this
model). According to the Indian model, there are four personality types. Some people are primarily reflective and use their
minds predominantly. Others are emotional. Another mode is
essentially active, while the last is experimentally inclined. In the
model we will use, I have used *emotional* for the path of the heart,
reflective for the path of the mind, and *active* and *experimental* for
the path of action. This model proposes that everyone has a certain personality style from which they see and react to the world.
It makes sense to go with strength of style so that the spiritual
personality type matches up to the path that is chosen.

The Path of the Heart

The path of the heart honors love above everything else. This kind of love is unconditional. It is not the kind of love many of us were raised with. "I will love you if" statements made when we were children left us with the impression that we could buy love with good grades or behavior. Conditional love leaves children in fear of messing up and being unworthy. Unconditional love, on the other hand, loves us constantly and consistently. This kind of love reduces fears, guilt, and anxiety. This love sees the love and beauty in all things and is always amazed at the beauty of God's creation.

Pure love comes from the heart. There is a profound difference between egoic love and spiritual love. If the eyes are a doorway to our hearts, it is always interesting to observe how we look at things. The ego always looks at the front of things it is interested in. This is the stare of acquisition and desire, and it is called ego vision. It does not involve the heart but is aligned with the animal brain. When meeting, people normally look at the area around the eyes first. This is where we get our first impressions of one another. Next, with egoic vision, we will often then size up one another based on appearance.

Spiritual vision works much differently. It is more like peripheral vision in that it takes in the larger area and looks beyond to see everything in a loving and inclusive way. Spiritual vision opens the door to our hearts. If you have ever been in the presence of a person using spiritual vision, you might have felt enveloped by his/her gaze, as if you were all that mattered. A person who uses spiritual healing has a calming effect on others; they feel loved and cared for in this person's presence. Spiritual vision is healing.

Spiritual love is not an emotion. It is a state of awareness and a way of being in the world. The context of love is set by *intention*. A working definition for intention is to have a purpose or plan and aim or direct the mind in that direction. As you know, intention can alter outcome. This occurs when conditions are right for the manifestation of the purpose or plan. Motive makes all the difference in the quality of the intention. For example, let's say I want to make more money. An egoic motive would be that I want to buy a nicer car to impress others. In this case, the intention is grandiose. However, if I want to make more money to help a family member who is having financial difficulties, my intention is virtuous. The question that must always be asked is, "Who is the thinker behind this intention?" Is it the ego or the Self? Does the intention arise from the animal desire to obtain more, or is it altruistic? Let the answer to this question be your guide. Always choose what conforms to the heart's love of others.

The path of the heart requires devotion, worship, and surrender. One devotes his/her life to selfless service. In this way, a person surrenders his/her life for the betterment of humankind by always acting from love. As one progresses on this path into the nonlinear realm of consciousness, the realization that there is no difference between giving and receiving becomes apparent. If we all are one, what we give to others we also receive. Sainthood may be the end result of this path. For example, Mother Teresa was able to see beauty in a population of society's outcasts: lepers, the homeless, the blind, and all those who were destitute and unloved. Just about everyone around her thought she was crazy at first, but she ended up winning the Nobel Peace Prize in 1979. Elizabeth Kübler-Ross, in her book *On Life After Death*, expresses the following: "Many people say: 'Of course, Doctor Ross has seen too many dying patients. Now she starts getting a bit funny.' The opinion which other people have of you is their problem, not yours. This is very important to know. If you have a clear conscience and are doing your work with love, others will spit on you and try to make your life miserable. Then ten years later, you are honored with eighteen doctorates for the same work. This is the situation in which I find myself."[39]

Walking a spiritual path is going against the flow and the status quo. There will always be those who will put you down, say you are using spirituality as a crutch, and ask you, "Why don't you get a real life?" Being a person of faith has traditionally brought persecution. It is no different today, especially in the West. These great women rose above the criticism and acted with great intention. It is their great love and integrity that stand as monuments to the power of the human heart,

---

[39] Kübler-Ross, *On Life After Death*, 9.

showing us the essential fact that nothing good in this world comes without love and compassion for ourselves and others.

The Path of the Mind

The human brain has evolved to favor survival in the natural world. It has adapted itself to finite objects and their meaning. God is infinite, completely different, and beyond the grasp of the mind.

In Huston Smith's book *The World's Religions*, our personalities are described using a theatrical metaphor. In the following description, he aptly tells us what goes wrong when we believe that our minds or egos (false selves) are really who we are. There are few who have his grasp of how the world's great spiritual traditions all lead us back to the real Self.

> . . . *for roles are precisely what our personalities are, the ones into which we have been cast for the moment in this greatest of all tragic-comedies, the drama of life itself in which we are simultaneously coauthors and actors. As a good actress gives her best to her part, we too should play ours to the hilt. Where we go wrong is in mistaking our presently assigned part for what we truly are. We fall under the spell of our lines, unable to remember previous roles we have played and blind to the prospect of future ones. The task of the yogi is to correct his false identification. Turning her awareness inward, she must pierce the innumerable layers of her personality until, having cut through them all, she reaches the anonymous, joyful unconcerned actress who stands beneath.*[40]

---

[40] Smith, *The World's Religions*, 30.

The mind path is often described as the path of nonduality or the path of negation. This particular pathway requires absolute humility and surrender. One surrenders everything to God, including his/her life. When all else has been surrendered to God, the only thing left is your very being. Surrendering your being or life to God is an invitation to Him to do with you what He will. Some have referred to this path as "no mind." In this pathway, it is necessary to surrender love of thinking for love of God.

Earlier, I compared the brain to a computer. Various types of information are uploaded into this computer. What we learn from our parents, religion, community, culture, and so on is stored on the hard drive. The programs for happiness are derived from this material. This material supplies us with our unique perspectives and is the basis of the ego. In order to get back to the true self—Self, or God within us—it is necessary to remove or surrender all of the thoughts, feelings, behaviors, and related opinions, motives, and character flaws from our hard drives to reveal the untainted processing unit—the Self.

The path of the mind involves meditation, contemplation, and spiritual study. To quiet the mind, it is essential to surrender all desire for thinking, as well as the illusion that our thoughts, feelings, and behaviors are valuable. For example, from an egoic perspective, an opinion can be viewed as a personal belief that has been emotionalized and made important because it is mine. It has no intrinsic value other than my delusion that it is somehow important. The Self does not have opinions but is built upon intention—to interface with the world, utilizing love, respect, and integrity for all living things.

By transcending the illusion of the "polarity of opposites," the nonlinear (nondual) realm can be reached. The paradox of opposites reveals the illusion that there are opposite aspects in life. For example, most people would say that cold is the opposite of hot and that dark is the opposite of light. In the world of oneness, cold is the absence of heat, not the opposite, and dark is the absence of light, not the opposite.

This path can lead to various degrees of enlightenment. With enlightenment, silence prevails as the "chatter" of the left brain disappears and one rests in the silence of the right hemisphere (see Chapter 9 on left and right hemispheres).

The Path of Action

All three pathways include action. Action involves perseverance or the ability to continue on the path even during the bleak times. Work is a form of action dedicated to the betterment of humankind and in the service of God. You can find God in the everyday world as easily as you can find Him in any other pursuit.

Sometimes along the spiritual trail, aspirants will reach a dry period where no matter how hard they try or how devoted they are, they seem to be stuck with no movement forward, or may even feel like they are going backward. This is not uncommon, and perseverance of right action and faith with hope are the keys to continuing on the journey.

Another form of action is self-discipline. Self-discipline demands that we stay on the chosen path without taking time off because we just don't feel like it today. The days when you least feel like you need to do your spiritual work are the times you most need the discipline.

Right action also involves "sticking with the winners" or in spiritual work "sticking with holy company." The Bhagavad Gita, the Hindu text with a written tradition dating back to approximately 500 years prior to Christ, and with probably several thousand years of prior oral history, is a beautiful eighteen-chapter poem. In the poem, Prince Arjuna carries on a dialogue with Krishna prior to battle. In the dialogue, Krishna answers many of Arjuna's questions about life and how to live it. A part of the dialogue involves what action is:

> One must learn well what is action to be performed, what is not to be, and what is inaction. The path of action is obscure. That man who sees inaction in action and action in inaction is wise among men; he is a true devotee and a perfect performer of all action. . . . [Krishna continues,] Those who have spiritual discrimination call him wise whose undertakings are free from all desire, for his actions are consumed in the fire of knowledge. He abandoneth the desire to see a reward for his actions, is free, contented, and upon nothing dependeth, and although engaged in action he really doeth nothing; he is not solicitous of results, with mind and body subdued and being

above enjoyment from objects, doing with the body alone the acts of the body, he does not subject himself to rebirth. He is contented with whatever he receives fortuitously, is free from the influence of the "pairs of opposites" and from envy, the same in success and failure; even though he acts he is not bound by the bonds of action. All the actions of such a man who is free from self-interest, who is devoted, with heart set upon spiritual knowledge and whose acts are sacrifices for the sake of the Supreme, are dissolved and left without effect on him.[41]

Krishna speaks of attachments because unhappy are those whose impulse to act is found only in the potential reward of that action. A repetitive theme in this book is that happiness can only be found through *selfless service* and not through *self-service*. One needs to be beyond success and failure and act, not according to old early-life egoic beliefs from family, community, and so on, but to follow what one believes with their heart to be right action. Remember, Jesus walked through boundaries throughout his ministry, asking us all to take right action and to not be swayed by the influence of that which we don't believe in our hearts.

---

[41] Vyasa, *The Bhagavad Gita* (Ann Arbor, MI: Border Classics, 2007), 18.

Alcoholics Anonymous and the Pathways

The pathway of Alcoholics Anonymous (AA), especially stated in Chapter 5, "How It Works," and Chapter 6, entitled "Into Action," utilize all three of the traditional pathways. The action component involves "taking the body and the mind shall follow." By the actions of going to meetings, meeting with our sponsors, and creating lists of those we have offended and made amends where to do so would cause no further harm, the recovering person's value and belief systems change as the neurobiology of his/her brain changes from that of an alcoholic or addict to that of a recovering person. The timber of the action changes from that of a "taker" with interest in self-service to a "giver" with an interest in selfless service. If one is to learn the path, it is necessary to learn it from others who have successfully walked the path, so "stick with the winners."

The pathway of the mind demands absolute humility and surrender. Radical humility is the only answer for afflictions of the narcissistic ego. AA reprograms the mind to appreciate the "here and now" without living totally in the past and future. "One day at a time" and "keep it simple" come to mind. As the first one hundred in AA came to believe, it is necessary to believe in something greater than your own ego, or recovery is doomed from the start. Trying to solve your problems with the same thing that created the problems—the ego—is a path doomed to failure.

AA has always been perceived as a heartfelt program where a desire to make others happy overrides selfishness. Working the twelve steps allows the aspirant to comply with the "golden rule" and to truly live in this world with serenity. This way of living is healing in that one is able to see the love and beauty inside of others when they cannot see it in themselves.

Page 57 in the Big Book summarizes what happens when one is single-minded in their pursuit of a better life: "Even so has God restored us all to our right minds. To this man, the revelation was sudden. Some of us grow into it more slowly. But He has come to all who have honestly sought Him."[42]

The Merging Paths

I am sure you noticed how all of these pathways overlap. Not only do they overlap, but they are interrelated. If one gives from the heart, his/her action will be pure and the mind right thinking. As one's path becomes more energized and advanced, the three pathways merge toward one consolidated path. I believe the paths start to merge at the level I have described as unconditional love or serenity. This nonlinear realization allows us to see everything as not only "one" but a product of God's love. When true spiritual enlightenment occurs, there is no distinction between the paths.

---

[42] *Alcoholics Anonymous*, 3rd. ed., 57.

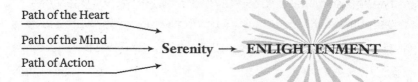

Path of the Heart

Path of the Mind   →   Serenity →   ENLIGHTENMENT

Path of Action

FIGURE 5.1. This diagram shows how the three paths start to merge as higher and higher levels of spiritual consciousness are achieved. All three become one at the level of unconditional love or serenity. In order to reach the state of enlightenment, one must receive a gift from God, as it cannot be achieved by one's own desire.

The Self is inseparable from the universe into which it is born. During the course of one's life, a person must build a work or magnum opus into which the three elements of heart, mind, and action are blended. Everything forms a single whole called Oneness. This creation continues over the life of the Self, and we serve to complete it even by the humblest of actions. We are instruments of God, living extensions of His greatness. We must unite ourselves with Him in the shared love of what we are working toward. As Teilhard de Chardin so beautifully states, "Our work appears to us, in the main, as a way of earning our daily bread. But its essential virtue is on a higher level: through it we complete in ourselves the subject of the divine union; and through it again we somehow make to grow in stature the divine term of the one whom we are united, our Lord Jesus Christ."[43]

Now we have a basic understanding of the terms and processes involved in the spiritual journey. The next step is to

---

[43] Pierre Teilhard de Chardin, *The Divine Milieu* (New York:Perennial, Classics, 1960), 27.

start the process of getting rid of negative energy, such as anger, rage, envy, jealousy, prejudice, and pride, which serves as the secondary gain of the ego. This is the start of disassembling the ego, the source of all suffering and misery in our lives.

We will also start the process of bringing into consciousness and surrendering the ego's unconscious programs for happiness. This will allow us to deflate the ego even further. As the ego is deflated, the Self starts to shine through in all of its radiance. Remember the formula: "Deflate the ego and the Self shines through."

6

Getting Rid of Resentments

*Though I speak with the tongues of men and angels,
and have not love in my heart, I become as sounding
brass or a tinkling cymbal. And though I have the
gift of prophecy, and understand all mysteries and
all knowledge; and though I have all faith, so that
I could remove mountains, and have not love in
my heart, I am nothing. And though I bestow all
my goods to feed the poor, and though I give my
body to be burned, and have not love in my heart,
I gain nothing. Love is long-suffering and kind;
love does not envy; love does not make a vain
display of itself, and does not boast; does not behave
itself unseemly, seeks not its own, is not easily
provoked, thinks no evil; rejoices not over iniquity,
but rejoices in the truth; bears all things, believes
in all things, hopes in all things, endures all things.*[44]

---

[44] 1 Corinthians 13:1–7, *Holy Bible*, trans. George M. Lamsa.

It is time to ask the important questions: Where am I in rela-
tion to God? Where am I in relation to myself? Where am I in
relation to other important people in my life?

When these questions are answered honestly, the spiritual
search for Self begins. God wants you to come out from hiding
and become intimate with Him. This is the honest path that
can take you on your spiritual journey. It is a difficult journey.
According to Luke 13:24, "Strive to enter through the narrow
door; for I say to you, that many will seek to enter in and will
not be able."[45] The path must be followed with rigorous honesty and a belief in something greater than our own egos.
Always remember that deep down in every man, woman, and
child is the fundamental idea of God. It may be obscured by
calamity, pomp, or worship of other things, but in some form
or other, it is always present. Faith in God and miraculous
demonstrations in human lives are facts as old as humankind
itself.

The old beliefs and ways of the ego are like unconscious
habits. When you acknowledge them and work with them, you
are bringing them into conscious focus. In the brain, unconscious material tends to move faster on the neuronal highways
compared with conscious material. That is because it is perceived in some way important to survival (which is what the
ego is all about). When we ask God to help us get rid of our
egoic suffering and misery, more often than not we will make

---

[45] Luke 13:24, *Holy Bible,* trans. George M. Lamsa.

mistakes trying to identify these old belief systems and make changes. This makes sense, as the slower conscious brain takes a while to catch up with the faster unconscious process. For example, let's say that I am envious of my best friend's girlfriend. The next time I see her, I will feel that envy. Envy is like gasoline to the ego. It feeds off of anger, envy, hatred, and prejudice. Over time, I will recognize the envy for what it is and start to change it to something like, "I am really happy for Ted that he has such an engaging girlfriend." This is far different than my ego saying, "Ted is such a dork; why does she like a guy like him?" (in other words, why doesn't she dig a cool guy like me?!).

What is happening here changes the neural system. When I don't reinforce old negative ways of thinking, feeling, and behaving, I can now build new neural pathways that can guide my future thinking, feeling, and behavior.

It is important to understand how the change process occurs. We can change based on changing our beliefs and the way we think. We can change by changing our behaviors. We can also change by working to change our feelings about people, places, and things. Whether we change emotionally, cognitively, or behaviorally makes little difference, because each influences the others. If I change the way I think, it will change the way I behave and feel. For example, maybe it is one of those nights when I am feeling a little down and really don't want to exercise. Taking the body and exercising (behavior) when it

seems disagreeable to me alone causes my feelings and thinking to improve. As each influences the others, they also create
physiological changes in neural wiring that support similar
behavior in subsequent similar circumstances. Continue to do
it over and over, and you have created a positive habit.

In order to change, spiritual tools are required to make the
necessary transitions. Acceptance, faith, and surrender allow
us to rid ourselves of self-defeating resentments and behaviors. As we accept ourselves as who we really are—the Self—
we begin to have greater compassion for ourselves. Remember,
without compassion for ourselves, we cannot have true compassion (unconditional love) for others.

Compassion gives us an inner serenity. It allows us to make
a commitment to an inner virtue such as kindness and stick
with it. Compassion allows us to see the love and beauty inside
others because compassion is a property of Self. Ultimately,
compassion opens the door to the understanding of the nonlinear "oneness" of all humankind.

I am most interested in how the ego is deflated and the Self
starts to shine through. What happens when one climbs higher
and higher up the mountain? How is this attainment of spiritual energy translated into good works? During this process of
change, how does the world look different to us, as opposed to
the way it used to look from a more egoic perspective?

As humans, we have become so used to misery, worry, fear,
anxiety, and conflict that they are believed to be the common

state of affairs. The ego is the cause for all of the negative energy we have stuffed inside of us. It has become accepted as normal to be angry, hurt, and remorseful. This is not the truth, however. We were born to happiness and love unlimited. This is the gift of Self. Without stripping away the ego, we can never move back to the nonlinear state where things just work out as they are meant to and we can live in peace.

The ego internalizes only the good and externalizes anything negative. Therefore, it can never be "my"—the ego's—fault. In any situation, this secondary gain keeps us from experiencing the pain of failure while projecting the negative emotion and personal attributes onto another person, place, or thing. The craftiness of the ego prevents personal pain but stunts opportunities for personal and spiritual growth. The ego is self-serving and is interested only in personal survival and gain. The ego is very tricky and operates in such a way that any failure is never its fault. I call this the secondary gain of the ego because it uses guilt, anger, envy, resentments, jealousy, and other negative emotions in the same way a car uses gasoline for fuel.

Spiritual transformation is all about discharging the negative energy and scaling back the ego to allow the Self to shine through. As the Self becomes enhanced, humility replaces pride. As the level of humility increases, the energy of pride and denial of the ego decreases. This allows us to view the world in a more truthful fashion. We move up the mountainside and can see the world around us more clearly.

EGO	SELF

FIGURE 6.1. A visual diagram of the formula: deflate the ego and reveal the Self. Every honored spiritual program uses this basic formula. As the Self is revealed, we become more humble and more teachable. We become students of the world.

Getting Rid of Secondary Gains of the Ego

The first place to start to rid ourselves of the secondary gains of the ego is to start with the negative emotions, such as anger, pride, prejudice, envy, greed, lust, and so on, often referred to as character defects. For example, I once had a client named Larry. He had a number of interpersonal failures with women whom he found desirable. He could not understand why these women could not see him as a desirable companion. He had a good job, was nice looking, dressed well, and had money and beautiful possessions, such as a large house and a fancy luxury vehicle. After they refused another date, he would be angry and wonder things such as, *What's the matter with her?* and *Doesn't she know what she is missing?* Sometimes it would take him days to get over the rejection. When I asked him what he got out of this, his response was essentially, "Not a thing, can't you see how much I am suffering?" and "Why is this happening to me?"

To take this concept just a little further, imagine that you had a first date with a narcissist who spent the entire evening telling you how wonderful he/she is and all of the great things in life he/she has accomplished. This person didn't bother to find out anything about you, because he/she was the only important person at the table. (This was Larry's problem.) The next time this person calls you up to go on a date, what are you going to say? Unless you are extremely codependent (the mirror opposite of the narcissist), you certainly would not want to spend another evening going out with someone so rude who had so little interest and regard for you. However, when you say "no" to this person, how will they handle it personally? That's right; just remember the secondary gains of the ego. Their anger will be directed at you and their self-talk will be along the lines of, "He/she doesn't know what he/she is missing." And "They weren't good enough for me anyhow!" or "What a loser; I am glad I am not wasting any more time and money here!"

When we look at the anatomy of this situation with Larry, it is easy to see that he was getting a lot out of these types of situations. First of all, it was not his fault, so he could get righteously indignant toward the other. Obviously, there is no opportunity for personal growth from this scenario, due to Larry's lack of empathy, which was secondary to his high degree of narcissism. Second, and most important, Larry can now use his anger to develop a seething resentment. This resentment now gives him carte blanche to do anything he wants, because it is not his fault. It was you that did this to him. Now he can go out and get drunk, threaten you, or take any other action he wants without blame. In some circumstances, such as during rage, his actions may well become addictive when he gets repeated high secretions of dopamine in his nucleus accumbens (reward center), giving his actions neuro-chemical reward. Yes, Larry was getting a lot out these nega-tive exchanges. Unfortunately, it wasn't what he needed.

It is not that difficult to get rid of secondary gains. There are three spiritual tools required. The first is *acceptance*, which allows us to bring the unconscious aspect of the secondary gain into consciousness. The second is *faith*, which allows us to believe there is a God who can rid us of these defects. The third is *surrender*, which allows us to let go of the ego's sec-ondary gain and turn it over to God.

How do you identify and bring into consciousness the unconscious ploys of the ego? It is the negative emotion that is the first clue. There are many situations that evoke anger, anx-iety, sadness, and so on. These are warning signs or red flags. When you find yourself feeling angry, prejudiced, envious, vindictive, and so on toward another person or due to a life sit-uation, examine the intention. Ask yourself, "Is my uncom-fortable emotion (anger, prejudice, greed, and so on) coming from my ego?" The answer will be yes, it is coming from your ego, and it will have to do with personal gain or perceived threat of survival. Ask yourself these questions:

Is this all about me with no regard for the other?
Am I feeling angry, hurt, depressed, or anxious
   because of the situation?

Is it something I want without regard to others?
Does it involve jealousy, prejudice, envy, greed,
selfishness, or place great importance on
material things and possessions?
And most important of all, am I feeling resentful
for not getting my way?

If you answer yes to any of these questions, your ego is involved in the situation. Obviously, there are certain situations where an angry response or feeling hurt is natural. For example, if people are driving fast and dangerously, it is natural to adamantly tell them to slow down as they are creating a dangerous, life-threatening situation with their irresponsible behavior. These types of situations are generally not about the worth of another, as you can still love them but be angry at what they do. This often happens with our children, where out of love we get angry at careless acts that might harm them. The bottom line, though, is always your intention. Ask yourself, "Is it about me or is it truly in another's best interest?" If the Self is involved, your desire will be to understand the other instead of being understood. It will involve true altruism, where the needs of others are carefully considered.

Acceptance

The second part of ridding ourselves of secondary gains now that they are in our conscious awareness is to accept

them for what they are. This is nothing more than the ego trying to get its way in the world. You can think of it as a little
child or unruly pet—at times hard to mange while at other
times quite amusing. The more you see the ego for what it
truly is—selfish—the more amusing it becomes. When you
can break the cycle leading to resentment and self-defeating
strategy, you will find yourself wondering, *How could I ever
have thought this way?* However, there is no need to cast judgment on the ego, for to do so switches focus from "you are
wrong or bad" to "I am wrong or bad." Really, it is the same
thought, as it dually places blame on one or the other.
Acceptance means I become aware of the secondary gain,
acknowledge it, and do not judge it or myself.

My favorite paragraph out of the Big Book of *Alcoholics
Anonymous* is one on acceptance. As a "taker" it was always "my
way" and it was "all about me." The arrogance of the ego led me
to believe that people should do and be what I wanted them to
be because I wanted them to. These old power and control
strategies are always doomed for failure sooner or later. If you
think about the millions of people in the world with that strategy, it is not hard to imagine the friction. Just imagine a cartoon
in which millions of people are running around with the bal-
loon caption saying, "No, let's do it my way!"

Acceptance makes us capable, adequate, and confident. It is
the beginning of the transformation of true spiritual consciousness. This transformation allows us to own our own

destiny by allowing for the understanding that we are responsible for our own happiness. No one else can do it for us! And for the first time, we start to internalize our powerful energy for positive change instead of relying on something or someone external to do it for us—a strategy full of repeated failure.

The story in the Big Book entitled "Doctor, Alcoholic, Addict" is one of my favorites because I can identify with it so strongly. The opening line is, "If there ever was anyone who came to AA by mistake, it was I." Several lines later it says, "Never in my wildest moments had it occurred to me that I might like to be an alcoholic." Later in the story, the author speaks about acceptance:

> . . . *acceptance is the answer to all my problems today. When I am disturbed, it is because I find some person, place, thing or situation—some fact of my life—unacceptable to me, and I can find no serenity until I accept that person, place, thing or situation as being exactly the way it is supposed to be at this moment. Nothing, absolutely nothing happens in God's world by mistake. Until I could accept my alcoholism, I could not stay sober; unless I accept life completely on life's terms, I cannot be happy. I need to concentrate not so much on what needs to be changed in the world as on what needs to be changed in me and in my attitudes.*[46]

The best thing we can do for the world is to grow up in the spiritual sense. As we grow, we take everyone else with us. As

---

[46] *Alcoholics Anonymous*, 3rd ed., 449.

we grow, we see the similarities, notice the wondrous, and love takes on greater meaning.

Later in his story from the Big Book, the doctor talks about his serenity being inversely proportional to his expectations. To live life without expectation of others or myself and to be able to accept people, places, and things just as they are is one of the secrets to happiness. Quite frankly, I have always had enough trouble just managing my own life, much less somebody else's. In a nonlinear world free from separation, there is no other; therefore, there is nothing to change. Everything is complete and just flows.

In the materialistic world of duality, everything is viewed from the perspective of the separate self, which causes us to automatically compare and contrast. This comparing and contrasting of ourselves to others leads us to blame, resentments, and self-pity, which then leads to misery and suffering. Once you accept things as they are, you realize the world is a very nice place to be and that the spiritual journey is always about truth. Revealing ourselves to ourselves and others frees us from having to hide from the world.

The ego loves getting you all worked up over what's not fair. It tries to convince you that it's important to prove yourself over and over again. This isn't true. One of the first aspects of acceptance is to know that you are perfect just the way you are. How could you be any other way in God's creation? With advanced spiritual consciousness, you learn how to love yourself, which is the prerequisite to loving others. There is no fault and no blame with acceptance. Acceptance is the opposite of the ego's perspective based on the premise that problems are caused externally by some person or situation. If I cannot accept myself and who I am and who I am becoming, then it will be difficult for me to accept others.

The Dalai Lama says, "Let me tell you what is wrong with the world. Look at children. Of course they may quarrel, but generally speaking they do not harbor ill feelings as much or as long as adults do. Most adults have the advantage of education over children, but what is the use of an education if they show a big smile while hiding negative feelings deep inside? Children don't usually act in such a manner. If they feel angry with someone, they express it, and then it is finished. They can still play with the person the following day. For me, that is the honest, natural way for basic human nature to act in such situations."[47]

Faith

The next step in the process involves *faith*. Do you have faith that God can take away the secondary gains of the ego if you surrender them to Him? Faith is something that you either have or you do not. Either God is everything or else He is nothing. God either is or He isn't. When you make the decision to

---

[47]http://blog.gaiam.com/quotes/authors/dalai-lama/46298.

turn all of your affairs over to God, how do you feel about the decision? Do you feel calm and confident, surrendering your very being to God, or do you feel indecisive when approaching surrender?

Faith is a radical reorientation of a life that worshipped personal power and control. There is no half measure with faith; you either have it or you don't. You can say yes or no to faith. If you say yes, this expresses a desire to expand, meet, and connect with life. Saying no protects us from being hurt by something that might not be there for us in the end. The power of yes and no are often damaged during childhood. As we started to believe in our manufactured ego, we interfaced with the outside world, vacillating between defiance and compliance, feeling compelled to please others, such as our parents, yet hating them for having to play what we defined as a game.

In any given moment, because you said no to faith yesterday, you are not doomed. You can say yes today. Also, because you acted in faith yesterday does not guarantee that you will not try to take back control today. Faith—because it is a way of being and not just a thought—happens always and only in a moment . . . each moment.

The Lord's Prayer has a part that must be thought about thoroughly. The words "Thy will be done" is a true testimony of faith. *Do you have total faith in God and do you surrender total control to Him? Can you do this with the understanding that it is His will and not yours? Do you really believe He will take care of you*

and that what comes to you in life is in your best interest either now
or later . . . maybe even for another lifetime? Can you hear the air as
it makes a shrill sound escaping through the crack in the ego's being?

Faith is a very human quality. James Fowler quotes the com-
parative religionist Wilfred Cantwell Smith: "Faith, then, is a
quality of human living. At its best it has taken the form of
serenity and courage and loyalty and service: a quiet confi-
dence and joy which enable one to feel at home in the universe.
And to find meaning in the world and in one's own life, a meaning that is profound and ultimate, and is stable no matter what
may happen to oneself at the level of immediate event. Men and
women of this kind of faith face catastrophe and confusion,
affluence and sorrow, unperturbed; face opportunity with con-
viction and drive; and face others with cheerful charity."[48]

Faith is a total alignment with heart and mind and is quite
difficult to maintain when at low levels of spiritual consciousness due to the ego's desire for control. As the spiritual
process moves forward, the right brain, which has regulatory
control over affect (feelings), aligns with its Creator. (See
Chapter 9 for further discussion on the left and right hemispheres of the brain.)

Faith is fundamental in our quest for transformation.
Complete faith is prerequisite to gaining the higher levels of
spiritual consciousness. Faith is not a separate dimension of
life. Faith is the orientation of the entire person toward living

---

[48] James Fowler, *Stages of Faith*, (New York: HarperOne, 1981), 11.

in this world and what living in the next realm might mean. Pure faith allows us to surrender everything to God's will— *Thy Will Be Done.*

Surrender

The last step in this process is to surrender the secondary gain to God. Surrender is about learning to live each moment of our lives without worrying about what we did in the past and about what will happen in the future. It involves the certainty of faith based in humility that each and every moment, one day at a time, is lived just the way it is supposed to be lived in order to learn the lessons we are placed on this earth to learn.

Surrender does not abdicate personal responsibility. I am still responsible for my life and—being faithful—I make a decision to allow something greater than me, something loving, to come into my life. I must be in action in this life, yet I surrender the results to God.

Spiritual surrender involves the admission that we are not in control of the outcomes of situations in our lives, as well as the understanding that it is now time to get out of our own way and let God guide and direct us. It involves being open to directions. This surrender gives us peace of mind as it points us in the right direction.

Spiritual surrender is also about releasing attachments and expectations. It is about being humbly attuned and unresisting to what is in store for us as we work our spiritual program. When we are attuned to God, we can effectively manage fear. Fear is the driving force behind the ego. However, fear only creates problems when we withdraw our surrender to God. By acting from the perspective of the Self, we do not honor the fear or let it deter us from our spiritual path. Surrender invites Divine Grace into our lives, whereby the underlying reality of the Self becomes progressively discovered as the ego dissolves.

There is no weakness in surrender. It is not about giving in to the wishes of another. It is about accepting the moment as it is and realizing there is Perfection in this moment. Surrender allows us to accept each moment for what it is as opposed to wishing for the moment to be different from what it is. More often than not, our egos want us to believe that the past "should not" have been the way it was and that we were deserving of something far better, or we should have made better choices. We also believe that the future will not be what it could have been because of what people or circumstances have done to us in our past. Our minds reflect over and over again how it *should have been* or it takes us into the future of *how it will be*. However, we cannot predict the future, for it is an illusion.

When we surrender everything to God, we are freed from other degrading forms of attachment, such as greed and desire for personal and interpersonal status. It is good to use the word "surrender" with commitment. In total commitment, nothing is held back from the Divine. It is a wholehearted giving of oneself.

Prayer can also be a form of surrender. At this stage, it may be more petitioning or supplication. Something like, "God, if you just get me out from under this burden I will never do it again. I know I have said this before, but this time I really mean it, God." This type of prayer is conditional and is based on the premise that if you give me what I want, I will believe in you. Over time, the intention to control God is given up and prayer becomes a dedication or willingness to be a servant of God and a channel for His will.

In summary, the most difficult part of dealing with old self-defeating behaviors, thoughts, and feelings is bringing their origin from unconscious to conscious awareness. The four-step process for getting rid of the secondary gains of the ego and dramatically reducing negative feelings, thoughts, and behaviors in your life is as follows:

1. Use the negative thoughts, feelings, and behaviors as a red flag and observe your intention.
2. As the unconscious process is bought into the light of the conscious mind, it must be accepted for what it is—an unconscious egoic process keeping us away from the love and joy of the Self in the moment.
3. Have pure faith in God, knowing with your heart and mind that He can take these burdens from you, reducing the power of the ego and allowing the Self to start to flourish within you.
4. Surrender the secondary gains to God, thus freeing all of

the negative energy associated with it from your being. This leaves more room for the Holy Spirit to do its healing work.

These steps allow us to free ourselves from the misery of self-defeating behavior. However, there is another layer we must deal with. Beneath the motives, opinions, character flaws, feelings, and thoughts of the ego is an even more unconscious set of processes taking place described as the ego's unconscious programs for happiness. These basic beliefs of the ego are the root cause of so much of our suffering. In the next chapter, we'll learn about these egoic unconscious programs and talk about how to get rid of them for good. This is the level of true healing that will truly deflate the ego.

7

Surrendering the Ego's Unconscious Programs for Happiness

Heavenly Father, we come before you today to ask your forgiveness and to seek your direction and guidance. We know Your Word says, "Woe to those who call evil good," but that is exactly what we have done. We have lost our spiritual equilibrium and reversed our values. We have exploited the poor and called it the lottery. We have rewarded laziness and called it welfare. We have killed our unborn and called it choice. We have shot abortionists and called it justifiable. We have neglected to discipline our children and called it building self-esteem. We have abused power and called it politics. We have coveted our neighbor's possessions and called it ambition. We have polluted the air with profanity and pornography and called it freedom of expression. We have ridiculed the time-honored values of our forefathers and called it enlightenment. Search us, Oh God, and know our hearts today; cleanse us from every sin and set us free. Amen!

—Billy Graham's prayer for our nation

Billy Graham's beautiful and timely prayer sees our human egos for what they really are—the source of our nation and the world's misery and frustration. Dr. Graham's prayer is a moral inventory for the many Americans who believe that "me first" is a birthright. The ego can justify anything, it seems, but "Woe to those who call evil good."

The problems we experience in life have nothing to do with God retaliating for our sins or the sins of our parents. God does not retaliate. The book of St. John 9:2–3 tells us, "And his disciples asked him, saying, 'Teacher, who did sin, this man or his parents, that he was born blind?' Jesus said to them, 'Neither did he sin nor his parents. But that the works of God might be seen in him.'"[49]

Life gives us wonderful opportunities to learn to grow beyond our mistakes and deficiencies. Unfortunately, the unconscious nature and multigenerational momentum of our jealousy, neglect, lust, greed, and blind ambition are slow to change direction. However, I believe this is in God's plan.

The ego is not a form of punishment. It evolved out of the Self and developed into a separate-self. The duality of the separate-self creates many problems in life. These problems are solved as one moves toward a nonlinear existence—that is, back to the Self.

We want to change for the better, to be better in the eyes of God. However, this is difficult when the ego unconsciously

---

[49] John 9:2–3, *Holy Bible*, trans. George M. Lamsa.

causes us to sin and experience suffering and misery. If sin means "to miss the mark," then to repent means we must change our direction and ways. In order to change, it is imperative to bring the old negative energy lodged in our bodies (the unconscious programs for happiness) into the light so that we can accept them for what they are and surrender them to God.

These old programs are not your fault. They are unconscious remnants of your childhood, information that has been internalized by a non-self-reflective brain during your early years. You might say it is your primary caregivers, culture, religion, nationality, and neighborhood doing the talking and thinking. The task at hand is to grow beyond these restrictions that are repeated over and over again in our misery.

Most people are deeply wounded within in some way or another. Certainly, science and psychology reduce symptoms and help people better cope with the problems attributed to early-life trauma. As a therapist I realized that I could not truly get rid of my own wounds, much less eradicate those of my clients. I came to believe that the only real and total resolution for these emotional wounds was to become that which I was meant to be. A return to the Self is the only way I know to get rid of the separation caused by the ego. It is this separation that is the base cause of our suffering. When we reside in the kingdom of God, there are no problems and there is no suffering.

When our needs for security, affection, and control are deprived, we compensate by looking for things outside of ourselves to give us pleasure, as if to artificially make us all right. Or if the pain is unbearable and we repress the energy of the memory into our unconsciousness, we end up replaying these old scenarios in painful ways throughout our lives. This is the start of attachment and the addictive process. Remember, everything is energy. The old hurts are negative energy stored in our bodies. This energy must be released for healing to take place.

Let's go back to our earlier discussion of the ego's programs for happiness—security and survival, affection and self-esteem, and power and control. Not having self-reflective consciousness prior to the age of about ten or twelve, we record in our brains the direct and indirect messages from family, community, religion, country, and so on. Some of the messages are negatively biased and hateful. Sometimes what is not done or said is as harmful, or even more so, as actual words or behaviors. Linear, dualistic understandings develop, guiding our thoughts, feelings, and behaviors throughout our lives. These understandings are a source of great misery and suffering, taking us farther and farther away from that which we are—our Self. Now add to this our instinctive desires for sex, food, and so on, which are so important for the many levels of survival, and imagine what goes wrong when the "reward center" gets hijacked by alcohol, drugs, excesses of sex, food, and other behaviors, like gambling and rage, which create incredible initial pleasure by greatly increasing the levels of the neurotransmitter dopamine.

For some of you it went like this: You were out of control in your early life. There was little affection and sometimes neglect or emotional abuse, and it seemed you could never do the right thing. In order to compensate you developed a rather grandiose egoic defense strategy, shielding you from the pain of never being okay. Now if you don't get your way and feel out of control, you get angry and resentful and blame the problem on the other person. It is miserable living in constant fear of not being good enough, and although you try to control everything, this also just leads you to misery. The instinct to engage sometimes kicks in and you get overtly angry with the so-called "offending party." Being "morally superior" gives the illusion of power and control, as well as promotes what is internally perceived as short-lived positive self-esteem. The instinct to avoid sometimes kicks in, and you find that alcohol or some other addictive substance, thing, or behavior can help you avoid the problem altogether. However, the negative energy is still inside of you. You might decide this strategy works well and your substance of choice feeds the false sense of being in control.

This is how character defects develop. The questions to ask are: *Who are the people, institutions, and principles that make us angry, resentful, and fearful because they will not let us have our way? What are the things we do—not out of altruism—so that people will think good things about us? How do we use others to help us create a (false) sense of security?* In understanding character

defects, it might help to understand their development as an egoic effort to do the best we can with what we have at the time. They are reactions to our trying to get our needs meet on a set of false assumptions about what our needs are. They are ways to try to find happiness without knowing what happiness is. The sheer craziness of it all is that the answer is right there inside of us as soon as we are brave enough to discover ourselves as God intended us to be. The pain of life itself and the many hurts contained during our years on this earth give us an opportunity to make enormous leaps along the spiritual path and up the mountain. This is why it is so wonderful to be human and to have every moment of our lives to make choices and changes for the good.

For much of our lives, we have been running from pain. As we get older, the game of hide-and-seek becomes more sophisticated. The hiding places are more secretive. Hide-and-seek becomes a metaphor for life. Instead of hiding, be counterintuitive and walk right into it, surrender it to God, and keep going forward. If you deny or avoid the pain, it will keep coming back to you in different ways, so why prolong the inevitable and the agony? For a way to face your pain, see the "Welcoming Prayer" on the next page.

Welcoming Prayer

When you are feeling angry, speak to the anger. Say, "Hello, anger. Welcome. Come on in and let me feel you." Fully feel the anger for a moment, then tell the anger, "Now it is time to go away. I have no time or need for you anymore." This counterintuitive way to handle any negative emotion—anger, anxiety, depression, and so on—can be extremely effective.

This technique comes from the work of Mary Mrozowski—a psychiatric hospital administrator and literacy volunteer in prisons. Welcoming Prayer redirects the emotional energy so that it is liberated from the egoic system and recaptured as vital energy for inner transformation. Don't let the negative emotion chase you from the presence of the moment. By embracing what you once repressed through acknowledgment, you disarm it, creating awareness.

Who Am I?

The spiritual life is the life of the Self. We have so often taken the easy way out. We are prone to welcoming everyone else's wrong solutions to the problems of life. We feel anxious because it is a symptom of our spiritual insecurities. At this stage, it is time to ask the question "Who am I?" I truly believe we have intuitive awareness of what the answer is, but the thought of radical change is scary. Just remember, there are no secrets in the universe. Consciousness knows everything that is truth.

Over time we enter a state of despair where we continuously deny and ignore both the questions and the answers to "Who am I?" Thomas Merton rings true when he says, "One of the moral diseases we communicate to one another in society comes from huddling together in the pale light of an insufficient answer to a question we were afraid to ask."[50] We are now asking the questions. It is easy to be philosophical or pseudoscientific and give clever answers to clever questions. But really, "Who am I?" We can even hide behind spiritual answers. While it is true that you are everything and you are nothing, this probably won't help you to move higher up the mountain unless you are truly willing to do the work to understand the nonlinear meaning of this statement.

Contemplation

When in the process of climbing the mountain, it is imperative to always have a safe base camp to return to. This is why it is important to maintain "holy company." Make sure you have a support system to help you along the way. If you do not like the idea of associating with groups of people working on spiritual growth, I understand that very well. Because I am some-

---

[50] Merton, *No Man Is an Island*, xiii.

what socially shy and introverted, a lot of my learning came from studying the words of the masters and applying them to my life while using contemplation to allow for a deepening of the meaning. Contemplation, to me, is applying your prayers to everyday practices in your life—at home, work, and school, and with yourself. Contemplation is not just saying the prayer but *becoming* the prayer in your living. Most spiritual texts recommend having a master or guru as a teacher. For myself, Jesus is my Master and his teachings in the New Testament are a basic source of guidance. As you move up the mountain, His words take on different meanings. Remember, Jesus was a nonlinear being and often spoke in parables with both linear and nonlinear constructs, depending on who had ears to listen and where they were in their own spiritual evolution.

Accepting our defects rather than denying them increases our self-esteem by reducing our defensiveness. It is rather infantile for people to think that they should always get their way. Most of us know or have known someone who had to get the last word in. These people are so driven to being right and getting their own way that their pride isolates everyone around them. Only a small child needs to win every time. Just by saying "I am sorry," most fires can be put out without any further damage. Again, we see the need to "grow up."

Our goal is to not reduce the impact of, but to totally take away, the unconscious programs for happiness. These programs are the basis for the thinking, feeling, and behavior (character) that cause us misery and suffering. This is not symptom reduction, but true healing at the level of the cause.

During the first centuries of Christianity, monastic, contemplative, and mystical traditions were a large part of Christian practice. This is especially true in the lives and the spirit of a fourth-century band of Christian renunciates known as the Desert Fathers. These spiritual zealots lived outside the boundaries of society, pursuing spiritual purification through the renunciation of all worldly distraction. They spoke of "resting in God," which means to "want what God wants" and not what the ego wants. Their legacy lives on today in contemplative Christianity.

I struggled off and on with meditative practices for almost thirty years. With irregular work schedules and traveling all over this country and others, it was at times difficult to have any sort of regular schedule. When I was not into a routine, I tended to feel guilty about it. Over the past years, I have become an irregular meditator, in that I do not have expectations of myself, and I meditate when it feels right. My approach has changed to a contemplative style of meditation. This started when I realized that my saying the prayer was not necessarily correlated with my living the prayer. To me, contemplation is about becoming the prayer in your life. My goal is to live my life like a prayer.

Contemplation allows us to discover the Self, as it is revealed within the infinite mercy and love of God. Contemplation is a response to a call from God. It begins the process of recovery of one's natural Self from the fragmented, self-centered, and frantic acquiring self. It starts with a search for the "One That Is" and leads to a discovery of the true Self within. With this, we start to resonate within our innermost self. This resonance is with the Self, and when it occurs, there is no longer any separation from "I Am."

Contemplation to me is spending time alone with God in the innermost parts of my being. This is where the most real and lasting works are accomplished in the depths of one's soul. It is a gradual interiorization (bringing within) of consciousness that allows me to move toward deeper levels of my own nature. It has given me a deepening of Self and an expansion in my capacity to understand and serve others.

The contemplative path is the most vibrant Christian path that I have found in regard to a path to Self. Besides the Desert Fathers' writings (such as those of John Cassian, ca. 360), other texts that were historically influential in contemplative Christian practices include *The Cloud of Unknowing* (written by an anonymous monk in the fourteenth century), writings by St. John of the Cross and St. Teresa of Avila, and works on *lectio divina* (Latin for "sacred reading"; see more on this in the next paragraph). In our times, the monastic, contemplative style of Christian practices was reintroduced in the 1970s by Trappist monks Fr. Thomas Keating, Fr. Basil Pennington, and Fr. William Meninger, who introduced the concept of "centering prayer." The basic discipline of centering prayer is to empty the mind and concentrate on the indwelling of God in silence.

Though many sources say the practice of *lectio divina* began in medieval times, other historians believe that it originated in biblical times in the early church. Over the past few years, it has been brought to our modern attention once again, and many who practice it are reaping the benefits spiritually. The basic form of *lectio divina* is: (1) a reading from scripture; (2) meditation; (3) prayer; and (4) contemplation. I utilize this approach by starting with a morning reading from the Bible. When something in the reading captures my attention, I will meditate, keeping the words as a focus for the meditation. This leads to spontaneous prayer followed by contemplation. Contemplation allows for a deepening of the words and concepts as the scripture or parts of it are unconsciously processed and on occasion come into the conscious mind throughout the day. With practice, this fourth step in *lectio divina* leads to the silent resting in God that is a result of centering prayer (we will take a closer look at centering prayer on page 252).

Contemplation is easiest for a child. As we grow, we lose the innate ability to be in the moment with God. Contemplation begins the process of recovery of one's natural unity with God (Self) from the compartmentalized, fragmented, acquiring self. It is a search for the One that leads to the finding of Self. To me, it is a love story and urges me to recall what Thomas Merton said: "We are what we love. If we love God, in whose image we were created, we discover ourselves in Him and we cannot help being happy: we have already achieved something of the fullness of being for which we were destined in our creation. If we love everything else but God, we contradict the image born in our very essence, and we cannot help being unhappy, because we are living a caricature of what we were meant to be."[51]

When we go into our secret places, it stops the outside noise and creates an inner silence. This inner silence allows the mind to "float" and free associate with the silence of God and the Holy Spirit as a backdrop, allowing for an interior rearrangement that happens over time. This might be best described as an "awakening."

Using a contemplative approach, the concept of having a divine therapist comes to mind. What if you accepted Jesus or God as your therapist? In this way, we can look at the spiritual journey as a form of psychotherapy designed to heal the old wounds of childhood. This journey would involve a purification of the unconscious—a true healing, as opposed to symptom reduction. *This is critical to remember: we are not working with the thinking, behavior, and feelings of the mind (ego), but the cause beneath these symptoms.* Utilizing acceptance and forgiveness as spiritual tools while continuing to surrender and to be honest and humble, the following plan of action can be implemented.

---

[51] Thomas Merton, *A Book of Hours* (Notre Dame, IN: Sorin Books 2007), 95.

Step 1: Affirming One's Basic Goodness (Self)

You are not the essence of your personality. In other words, you are far greater and more valuable than your thoughts, feelings, behaviors, and failings. You are so much more than what others have said you are. There is no such thing as a "loser"—only those who choose to stay lost. Because of the Divine Love of God, there is no human condition that cannot be healed and/or forgiven. God is not asking you to earn anything. It is enough to become that which you are—the Self. We have acted based on early-life belief systems. Some of these are true, and some of these are false. Unfortunately, our childish minds were incapable of telling the difference. Also, the identification and overidentification with these unconscious programs for happiness depends on other people and situations to make us happy. This makes our happiness nearly impossible to fulfill. Finally, the idea that we are unlovable, unworthy, or a failure is an insult to God. We are created in the image of lovability; one who is innocent and able to embrace change. Therefore, the image to be accepted is:

- We are lovable.
- We deserve happiness and joy; it is our birthright.
- Nothing that we have done is unforgivable in God's eyes.

Step 2: Becoming Aware of Our Beliefs About the World

Step 2 often starts with a spiritual opportunity, but it can begin at anytime in life. Some people have told me that when their children had grown up and moved out, the time and energy for self-exploration presented itself. Any opportunity where the ego is overwhelmed—such as an existential crisis, loss of a loved one, addiction, depression, or serious medical problems—can serve as the stressor that facilitates willingness for change. At this point, we are willing to look at the support systems (beliefs due to the unconscious programs for happiness) that keep the ego in control. These support systems can be released by:

- Reducing and eliminating our attachment to the unconscious programs for happiness.
- Reducing attachment to our overidentification with the various groups we belong to. It is wonderful to have good friends and family, but overreliance on everything they tell us is naïve.

At this stage, we must develop the willingness to look honestly at ourselves and start the process of identifying unconscious, self-defeating programs and questioning what our nation, religion, neighborhood, culture, and so on has told us about what is good and what is bad and—as important—who is good and who is bad. At this point we need to start to understand who we are and what we believe about the world we live in.

This is one of Jesus's messages in the New Testament. Jesus knew who he was and did not allow others to sway him from what he knew was right. He ate with tax collectors and hung out with prostitutes and Samaritans. I believe he was telling us not to take the general opinion but to find out for ourselves. Distillation allows us to separate our essence from what others tell us is correct about ourselves and our world. The question to ask is "What is right for me?" In the end we must learn to be true to ourselves and act based on what we believe, not what the group we hang out with believes. This is what I feel we will be judged by.

The energy creating the willingness for change is so often pain related. When we can see no other easy door to walk through, pain motivates us to change and to find out who we are. Step 3 will help us move close to the Self.

Step 3: Dismantle the Emotional Programs to Heal the Problem

There are two primary strategies involved in dismantling the egoic unconscious programs for happiness. The first—just like working with secondary gains—involves using negative emotion as a red flag. The second is a deeper practice utilizing unfocused meditation such as mindfulness and, especially, centering prayer. Both strategies are even more effective when used together.

Strategy No. 1: Use Negative Emotions as Red Flags

Simply notice a negative emotion that you are currently feeling, such as anger, envy, jealousy, prejudice, procrastination, or greed. Write that emotion down on a piece of paper. Also record what triggered the emotion. What was the particular event, person, or memory that immediately preceded the emotion you are currently experiencing? Now, identify which unconscious program(s) is the source of your negative feelings. (Refer back to Chapter 2 for details regarding the ego's unconscious programs for happiness.) If the program is security and survival, you are facing the fear of aloneness and disconnection. If the program is affection and esteem, you are facing the fear of unworthiness. If the program is power and control, you are facing the fear of losing safety and control.

Next, reflect on how many times this program(s) has caused you suffering and misery. Remember, it will take a while to learn to catch yourself from automatically falling back into the same dilemma. Accept and surrender each unconscious program to God. This frees up the energy stored in the body and allows it to depart as opposed to playing hide-and-seek and repressing the negative force. Notice that as the energy departs, you may feel anger, sorrow, or other emotions, and they may be accompanied by physiological responses, including tears.

Each time you catch yourself falling back into the old pro-gram, install a healthy response, such as telling yourself, "I don't need to act this way anymore, and I surrender the nega-tive emotion and the egoic unconscious program for happiness to God." You could also say a brief prayer, partake in a short meditation, excuse yourself from the situation for a while, put a smile on your face, or figure out how you can make the most of the situation. With practice, this new response will become your new unconscious way of dealing with similar situations.

Strategy No. 2: Engage in Centering Prayer

Unfocused meditation is the preferred form. This type of meditation works predominantly through the right hemisphere of the brain. Spiritual growth causes a movement from the left hemisphere to the quiet and serenity of the right hemisphere. (See Chapter 9 for more on this.) Since I am utilizing a contem-plative Christian approach, we will focus on centering prayer.

Centering prayer commits us to the liberation of uncon-scious character flaws. It puts us in the presence of God and consents to His working within us to free us from the suffering caused by the ego's unconscious programs for happiness. Remember, the deflation of the ego is the mechanism whereby the Self shines through in its radiance. It has meaning because it expresses our pure intention to open up to God and allow Him to remove our human misery.

There is no other security except the security of God.

Centering prayer involves giving all of our power over to our Creator. It involves an emptying of oneself so that the Holy Spirit can shine forth. Emptying ourselves allows us to receive real unconditional love (affection) and perfection (esteem), which leads us to freedom and happiness.

Life should be a continuous "dying to self," giving up the ego to discover the Self. It involves a willingness to give up what I want in order to create a space for the Holy Spirit. Dissolution of the ego is not achieved by guarding the purity of our beings but through the radical relinquishment of everything. Jesus gave himself fully into life and into death. His was a love given through complete vulnerability. Ironically, the pathway to happiness coexists with giving ourselves away. Self-service becomes the key gesture for creating meaning and purpose in our lives.

With centering prayer, healing is experienced on an energy level. When the body's tension is reduced, it releases stored negative energy, allowing painful and forgotten memories to come to the surface. One must face these emotionally painful memories and feel them. After this, surrender all of the negative emotional energy to God and allow yourself to be filled with the Holy Spirit. Obviously, it is imperative that one believes in the healing power of the Holy Spirit. It is also important to remember that this phenomenon occurs over time and through practicing the centering prayer technique.

Centering prayer involves a "resting in God." The silence

behind everything is the first language of God and is where we seek to rest. The first thing the practitioner wants to do is pick out a sacred word. This should be a very short word of no more than two syllables. I like the word *Abba*, the Hebrew word for "father," which Jesus used when talking to his heavenly Father. Others to consider are Jesus, God, love, faith, silence, peace, or mercy.

Make sure the word you choose "fits" comfortably when you say it silently. Also, when in your meditative stance, be sure that you are comfortable. Then, introduce your sacred word into your meditation. This word is to be used very quietly and gently when thoughts or feelings interfere with the quiet. This is all you need to do. Just experience the calm, peace, and serenity as you rest in God. Don't worry about doing this correctly, as there is no wrong way to communicate with God if you are sincere and loving in your approach.

While it is recommended that the practice should be instituted twice a day for twenty minutes each time, I have found that even once a day can be effective. During centering prayer, I have begun to cry without knowing exactly why. If this happens or anything similar happens, just let it go and surrender the feeling to God. Sometimes I will have a big smile on my face. It is nice just to stick with this. Other times, a memory flashes into consciousness, and, if appropriate, I ask for forgiveness and surrender it to God. Many times nothing comes into conscious awareness, and I just enjoy the peace and quiet of consciousness.

If you have experienced severe life trauma, the energy, as it is released, may be overwhelming. Generally, the energy rises slowly over time, but sometimes it comes on with greater force. If you find yourself becoming very uncomfortable (extreme anxiety and/or depression) or having thoughts of hurting yourself or of using alcohol or other drugs, stop the practice immediately. In these instances, seek the help of a professional clinician. No technique works for everyone, and the most important thing is to do no harm to yourself or others.

If you are more advanced in your spiritual work, you may experience the rising of kundalini (energy) coming up from the base of the spine, through the backbone, and toward the head. This is an ecstatic feeling. My body has quivered all over during such an experience. Of course, everyone is different, so there is no particular right or wrong experience. The important point is to use the practice to deepen your faith in God's abiding presence and familiarize yourself with the first language of God: silence. The benefits of this practice will be experienced in daily life, as you might find yourself more accepting of situations that in the past caused you to overreact emotionally.

The work involved in letting go of the secondary gain of the ego and ridding oneself of the ego's unconscious programs for happiness allows us to get rid of the negative energy and self-defeating unconscious patterns that have caused so much suffering and misery in our lives. We allow God to be our

Therapist. In the upcoming chapters, you will learn techniques that you can use to increase your positive spiritual energy and find greater joy and happiness in your life. After all, they are your birthright.

8

Continuing on the Spiritual Path

Amazing grace, how sweet the sound,
That saved a wretch like me.
I once was lost but now am found,
Was blind, but now I see.

'Twas grace that taught my heart to fear.
And grace my fears relieved.
How precious did that grace appear
The hour I first believed.

Through many dangers, toils, and snares
I have already come;
'Tis grace that brought me safe thus far
and grace will lead me home.[52]

---

[52] John Newton, "Amazing Grace," accessed online at
http://www.constitution.org/col/amazing_grace.htm.

In Chapters 4 and 5, we explored the spiritual concepts of consciousness, spiritual transformation, and so on, and the traditional paths (heart, mind, and action) that are useful for navigating the spiritual journey. Now we will take a closer look at each of these concepts as we continue on the spiritual journey.

Now that you have rid yourself of much of the negative unconscious material holding you back from receiving the joy and love that this life has to give, it is time to move along the path and up the mountain. Getting rid of all of the negative energy allows you to leave base camp without the old heavy burden placed upon you by the impossibility of living up to what others told you life should be. This is the beautiful part of the journey, as you gain an appreciation for the love and beauty residing in everything and in everyone. Still, this incredible journey will demand much from you—first and foremost, single-mindedness of purpose.

You will find your mind contemplating the journey throughout your waking day and, for some, even in your dreams. The journey—not the destination—becomes the driving force of your life. As mentioned earlier, if you feel yourself being pulled toward greater spiritual understanding, you are on the uphill climb, coming closer and closer to your true Self. Avoid making enlightenment or some other achievement your goal, as it will keep you in the duality of now and the future, as you constantly compare where you are to some illusion of where you think you need to be. The journey stays in the focus of the moment and the experiences of personal spiritual understanding. The fourteenth-century work by an anonymous monk, *The Cloud of Unknowing*, gives a wonderful metaphor for the experience of being in the moment. The monk advises a neophyte to always focus above himself to the "cloud of unknowing" (God, which we are not capable of seeing or understanding) and to try to be in the moment and open to understanding the Divine while staying above the "cloud of forgetting," which represents all worldly matters.

The gifts of the Divine, such as unconditional love, wonder, gratitude, forgiveness, and other positive emotions have a profound effect on the brain. When we are filled with love, acceptance for the other, and gratitude, we can facilitate the same neurobiological response in another. You are a healer and your presence is healing if you resonate with the other's right hemisphere. We will look at the changes in greater detail in Chapter 9, but for now let's appreciate the process.

Have you ever trembled in awe? Have you unexpectedly experienced human kindness when least expecting it? When expecting to be rejected, have you ever received unconditional love? If anything like this has happened to you, you understand well the nature of a numinous experience—in other words, you know what it is like to be filled with the sense of the Divine, or holiness. Plato described this phenomenon when he wrote, "First a shudder runs thorough you, and then the old awe creeps over you." This blend of mystery, ecstasy, and the numinous is described beautifully in Rudolph Otto's *The Idea of the Holy*, which I recommend for further reading.

FIGURE 8.1. This diagram shows the neurobiological cycle leading to spiritual growth based on Ernest Rossi's novelty-numinosum-neurogenesis effect. The diagram is taken from my training entitled "The Art and Science of Healing" and was adapted from a similar figure created by Rossi. This synthesis implies that the helper/healer has power to effect change in another and that change is not some internal process only occurring within the other.[53]

The numinous experience is a sense of awe that garners the attention of our conscious brains due to their novelty. Novelty lights up the conscious areas of our brains. For example, what if everything seemed to be going wrong with your life and no matter how hard you tried, you seemed to become more and more depressed? You think that your friends no longer want to

---

[53] Ernest Rossi, *The Psychobiology of Gene Expression* (New York: W. W. Norton, 2002), 139.

be around you, and you start to believe you are just plain unlovable. You see a therapist who specializes in your particular problem, and she receives you with unconditional love and caring. For the first time in a long while you feel safe and cared for. This type of experience motivates our lives, which leads to a change in gene expression.

That's right—love, caring, and acceptance can change the way our brains work. Genes produce proteins that are the building blocks of much of our bodies, including the nervous system. During gene expression, psychobiology integrates experiences of the mind (the numinous, loving experiences) with biology (gene expression and protein synthesis) to create neurogenesis (epigenesis). Epigenesis is brain growth involving genetic change that has been created or influenced, in this case, by the external environment of caring. It is neurogenesis (epigenesis) that leads to healing on a neurobiological level.

The next stage is from neurogenesis to consciousness. This involves neural networks being "reformed" or "recontextualized" into new configurations with new meaning (a more aware or spiritually evolved mind), which then leads to healing and higher levels of consciousness called *transformation*. Spiritual transformation involves neurobiological changes in the brain structure and networking. The world now looks different to us, although it has not changed. We have climbed a little higher up the mountain.

Let's go back to the example of being kind to everything and everyone, including yourself. Earlier I mentioned that I made a commitment to be kind without failure in this manner for a period of eight weeks. After eight weeks, it became nearly impossible for me to get angry at another. To do so caused me great pain, as the neurobiology of my brain had changed. This is another example of how our brains change to support spiritual growth and understanding.

Andrew Newberg in *How God Changes Our Brain* describes how one can learn to become more compassionate. Compassion involves empathy and the ability to resonate with another, as well as respond to the pain of the other. The anterior cingulate cortex (a part of the prefrontal cortex) plays a key role in compassion in that it helps to keep a balance between how we are thinking and the resulting emotions we experience. Newberg's imaging studies showed that a strong frontal lobe stimulates the anterior cingulate cortex and reduces firing in the amygdala, an area associated with anger and fear. Meditation and spiritual practices such as compassion for all living things strengthens the anterior cingulate. This guides us toward positive emotions such as love, acceptance, and compassion. If we continuously practice spiritual principles, the stronger the anterior cingulate will become and the more compassionate you will become. The more a person focuses on love and compassion toward self and others, the stronger the brain's "compassion circuit" becomes and the easier it is to feel compassion and to help others reduce their personal pain.

Higher levels of consciousness allow for what can be called an "aware" mind. As we move away from the focus of the ego and its desire for personal gain and self-interest, we develop what has been described as "knowingness." The higher our level of consciousness becomes, the higher our level of "knowingness," which gives us a better understanding of the essence of things (as opposed to the appearance). We can see the whole and not just a small part. We start to see through the silliness of other people's "games" and the "hooks" of mass-media advertizing. This understanding generally allows us to see through life's illusions and to become more easygoing and mellow. As the short form of the Serenity Prayer exclaims, "Lighten up!" and wear the world like a light garment.

In order to continue to develop an "aware" mind, it is very important to continue to read, pray, meditate, and contemplate our journey here on Earth and to deepen our understanding of our mission. In order to grow and exceed the challenges of life as we live it, we must take the time to study, learn, and allow this information to incubate into true knowledge and wisdom. One way of thinking of this change is illustrated in Figure 8.2 on the following page.

Change also represents an exchange. We exchange the misery of the egoic self for a more joyful and loving way of life. Change also involves empowerment. Getting out of the rut of our old lifestyles, we now have new choices. Now we can decide who we really are. Change is a process. It takes time. Spiritual change often happens in an unpredictable fashion.

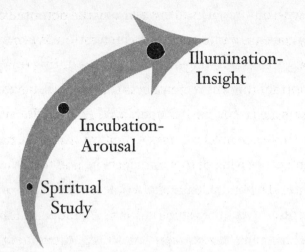

FIGURE 8.2. When incubated over time using prayer, meditation, and contemplation, continual spiritual study allows for the continuance of spiritual insight and growth or illumination. Illumination leads to spiritual transformation and movement up the mountain.

Finally, change occurs on many levels. When the opportunity to change is first presented to us, it rests in the cranial area. The brain/mind works with the issue to look at what change might mean to us. Most of the brain works in a reductionist fashion, meaning we break the issue down into its tiniest parts so that they can be analyzed. This tendency of the brain disallows us to see the change from the perspective of the bigger picture. We get caught up in the detail of change. This is a form of paralysis by analysis. Stepping back, we can grasp the change as an essential part of the larger contextual picture.

Initially we are caught up in gathering information and

dealing with our initial intuitive sense of the potential change. Now change enters into a period of incubation. We may not be conscious of what is going on in our brains during this period. The important thing to remember is that once we have opened up a new issue in our spiritual/personal growth, the brain will work on this issue until it gets the right information, has completed the processing of this information, and has reached its conclusion. The brain demands closure.

In spiritual work involving nonlinear understanding, the process of incubation seems to allow the movement of the awareness away from the mind and toward the heart. This interval of time is a period of profound creativity. At some point, we may have a breakthrough. We often call these "epiphanies," and they are not always present to us in words. Quite often, the heart knows the answer, and we feel the change in us as it settles into our chests. It is almost like being overcome by the answer. In my experience, at the moment of illumination or clarity, I feel a physical sensation as if the answer has just settled into my heart. These illuminating "aha" experiences are moments to revel in, and this is how change happens on the spiritual trail. You can know something rationally, but until there is congruence between heart and mind, there is still the nagging feeling of incompleteness.

Reductionist functioning is a left-brain task in which everything is broken down so our egos can compare and contrast. This process is separate, isolative, and alienated from everything else. On the other hand, the right brain is intuitive and connected to the infinite field of consciousness. However, holistic functioning, in which the whole brain works, gives us an overall sense of satisfaction as being part of the world. It is about the unified whole and interconnectedness. Spiritual experiences rely on holistic functioning. They are non-language-based and are involved in transformation, allowing us to sense and have knowingness about ourselves and how we relate to the world.

We now have a sense of personal integrity that has opened itself to the ultimate power of the Holy Spirit, for which nothing is impossible. Christ said, "Be perfect. Become perfect." It is possible to be perfect because he was perfect. We cannot do it by ourselves, but we can accomplish this in him. It is possible to be perfect because of the gift of God's love manifested in His son Jesus. We can also choose not to be perfect because we can refuse the gift of His unconditional love. When we refuse the gift, we have to rely on some theory of philosophy or theology to explain how the ego cannot be transcended. It is possible to be free of the ego, but we are still part of the mystery.

The most difficult task is to move from the linear (dualistic) to the nonlinear (nondualistic) nature of reality. Remember, it is the ego that resides in the linear world while the Self is non-linear. To be able to accept the world as perfect is nearly impossible for the dualistic mind. This egoic mind calculates what is good and what is bad about everything and everyone.

People with unconscious programs oriented toward power and control cannot deal with the uncertainty and lack of concreteness of the nonlinear realm.

Nonlinear awareness cannot be reached by just using the mind. As a matter of fact, the mind gets in the way. Our whole process of education has led us to believe that everything worthy is of the mind and its calculating intelligence. The dualistic mind sees everything as separate. The nonlinear mind sees everything as "one." In "oneness" there is neither aloneness nor isolation; we are all attached to one another as a part of the energy field called consciousness (zero-point field, Holy Spirit). In the nonlinear realm, everything is as it should be and so all is okay. This is because there is no looking to the future, which is the mother of expectations. Without expectations, nothing can turn out the way it is not supposed to. This is the realm of unconditional love and acceptance. It is understanding that love is not a feeling but is a way of resonating with everyone and everything in the world. This is to really be alive!

In order to move toward a nonlinear reality, I would suggest trying some or all of the following activities. Be very careful of technique. Technique alone can sometimes just polish up the old consciousness and not help you break through into a new nonlinear consciousness. What you are looking for is a deeper understanding, not some egoic embellishment. Some people just jump from one set of techniques to another. Find a path that is well worn by those who have reached a higher state of awareness and stick with it. Search for truth using just your mind, and you will find there are no fixed answers; when you quit the struggle to find answers in this dualistic world, you are now ready to start the real journey. Just let go of everything you think you know and become like a child, full of curiosity and wonder. It makes no difference how long one has been in darkness; as soon as the light is turned on, it will chase away the darkness. Be teachable. Try the following:

- **Quit using the words "I," "me," or "mine" so frequently:** Your whole life you have identified yourself as "I" or "me" and everything you own as "mine." However, these three words are products of the ego (the separate self). "I" is a self-righteous actor showing the world only what the ego wants to be seen: I am perfect and all fault is external. The "me" reacts and things happen to it as it suffers due to outside events: *Why does this always happen to me?* "Mine" is possessive and is the province of the grasping, greedy, and clinging self. Whatever is possessed also possesses, so "mine" winds up as its own captive. By possessing more, it has more to lose: *Those are mine and I need more to be all right.* The ego is an illusion. If you stop supporting it, it will fade and more of your Self will shine through.

- **Quit making judgments and constructing opinions of others and situations:** The ego loves to compare and contrast. This keeps us separate from others. As a matter of fact, the ego is addicted to thinking. If we can learn to witness our thoughts instead of giving them credibility, it would seriously diminish the ego. Think how often and how much time one spends constructing opinions of others. Motives and opinions originate from some duality. For example, "This is what I think and I am right and you are wrong." Just appreciate the fact that all people are perfectly where they should be on their own personal journeys. If you want, you can understand they are where they are on their journeys and have a ways to go, and then wish them God's blessing.

- **Notice the paradox of opposites:** The ego sees everything from the perspective of difference. For example, *I have white skin and you have brown.* In the nonlinear world, there is no such thing as opposites. In Chapter 4, we mentioned that dark is not the opposite of light; it is only the absence of light. Look for sameness and relationships in everything. We are "one."

- **See the beauty in all things:** Everybody and everything is on a journey—a perfect journey—back to our source. Strive to see beyond right and wrong, observing that all are doing the best they can with the situation life has delivered to them and the tools they have to cope. No one is any better or any worse than anyone else. How can we be better than another if we are all one?

- **Pick out a conundrum:** As stated earlier, mine was how can I love someone unconditionally who blows up a busload full of children? I could quote you a Bible verse about loving your brother as you love yourself, but, as mentioned, at the end of the day I still felt like killing the SOB. Finally, out of consciousness came the feeling of love sinking into my heart, and although I have difficulty putting what happened into words, from that point on I grasped the true meaning of "oneness." We both have the same Creator. It is God's task to judge and not mine. When I judge I am playing God.

An illustration of the concept of spiritual transformation can be seen in *The Bhagavad Gita*, when Krishna is asked to describe a wise and devoted man. He responds:

> *A man is said to be confirmed in spiritual knowledge when he forsaketh every desire which entereth into his heart, and of himself is happy and content in the Self through the Self. His mind is undisturbed in adversity; he is happy and contented in prosperity, and he is a stranger to anxiety, fear, and anger. Such a man is called a Muni. When in every condition he receives each event, whether favorable or unfavorable, with equal mind which neither likes nor dislikes, his wisdom is established, and, having met good and evil, neither rejoiceth at the one nor is cast down by the other. He is confirmed in spiritual knowledge, when, like the tortoise, he can draw in all of his senses and restrain them from their wonted purposes.*[54]

This description is of one who has moved well into the non-linear realm of existence. We live in this dual world—a world

---

[54] Vyasa, *The Bhagavad Gita*, 11.

of "material things" and a world of "inner meaning." When the spiritual aspirant has raised himself/herself to a point where the material world has lost much of its importance and becomes secondary to the inner meanings, then he/she has become a spiritual person. Spirituality lifts us from one who responds to material ambitions to someone who is pulled in the direction of spiritual transformation.

When you climb the mountain, the mountain will test your endurance, resolve, patience, and, most of all, your faith. Depending on where you are on the mountain, these tests will be quite different. There are moments when you think you don't have enough to give. And there are moments when you seem to be doing all of the giving but not getting anything in return. There are slopes that are steep and areas to be traversed that seem easier. All in all, you get from the climb what you put into it. The rarefied air of the mountain deflates the ego. In exchange, you receive your Self. The mountain demanded your grandiosity and arrogance, but it gave you back humility and acceptance. This realm is nonlinear and demands a different understanding about life and how it should be lived. It is about becoming what you were intended to be. It is about the search for "Home."

Nonlinear Awareness Versus Enlightenment

Many seem to confuse nonlinear awareness with the term *enlightenment*. Enlightenment exists in the nonlinear realm but is a more advanced state of awareness. There are millions of people who have reached a nonlinear understanding, but only a small handful of people who reside in a permanent enlightened state. To grasp nonlinear reality, we grasp that we are part of the All. Enlightenment is to become one with the All. Enlightenment is wisdom or "knowingness" that goes well beyond reason and comes from mastering this world. An enlightened individual does not exist as a "me" or an "I." He or she is no longer of this world and is detached from it. The ego is reabsorbed back into the Self, and there is total silence in place of what was the "chatter" of the brain. An enlightened being has experienced the painful demise of the ego as it puts up its last stand for unique survival. Enlightened souls pass into the "light" and do not come back to what they were previously (such as what happens in a near-death experience).

Enlightenment is the revelation of the Holy Spirit. Its energy is so powerful that one in the "light" cannot speak or move, and this can exist for some time. Enlightenment has a number of degrees. If you pass through the "void," you might experience a sense of evil, which, in actuality, is the absence of God's love. To pass through the void and arrive on the other side is to be one with God's love. It is such a powerful, dramatic experience and is much differentiated from achieving nonlinear awareness. However, nonlinear awareness is a wonderful place to be. It is full of joy and happiness and a love for all of humankind. In order to move toward enlightenment, you must be willing to surrender everything, including joy, happiness, and even your life, as you understand it.

Maybe the greatest gift is the understanding of the divine paradox that tells us in order to be happy we have to be of selfless service to others. We must "give it away to keep it." What must we give away? The answer is the essence of our Self— Love. That is the divine paradox. Giving love means receiving love. In the nonlinear world, giving and receiving are one and the same because you and I are one. It is satisfying to know that God exists and you are one with, and therefore inseparable from, Him.

If the love and happiness radiating from an infant are reflected back to the child from the parent, the infant feels secure. This infant is the embodiment of Self. At this point, he/she is reasonably undisturbed by the pettiness of the material world. Soon enough, the material world encroaches upon each individual and shatters the innocence and trust. The spiritual path gives us an opportunity to move back toward the experience of the child. I have a Buddhist friend who asked me one day, "What is the purpose of the ego?" I replied that it is a trail of bread crumbs that we can follow back to where we started. And, in fact, that is the spiritual opportunity.

I know that I have said this a number of times, but the

spiritual journey is not about acquiring or adding anything. *It is about getting rid of the opinions, character flaws, and motives of the ego, thus allowing the Self to fully reveal itself in our lives.* When you have reacquired this radiance, you truly understand unconditional love and selfless service. When you give back to the world, whether it is a subjective experience or material object, you get to enjoy it during the anticipation, the act of giving, and during the aftermath of the giving process.

The greatest gift is the gift of your Self. The most beautiful gift is the Love freely given from you to another. This, to me, is the essence of unconditional love. I heard this story from a flight attendant at Los Angeles International Airport (LAX). It happened that a flight attendant in early recovery from alcoholism was exiting her flight when she was overcome with an urgent craving to drink. She thought, *I will find a bar and have a few before I go home.* In a moment of clarity, she realized the dangerous state of her mind and immediately went to an LAX pager phone and asked for the following message to go out over the intercom, "Will any friends of Bill W come to Gate 10?" Within minutes, there were fifteen men and women sitting with her at the gate. Two of them had gotten out of their boarding line and would miss their flight to honor the promise to be there if anyone struggling with their addiction was in need. This is true love. This is the Self shining through. It is the kind of love that brings tears to the eyes and a warm feeling deep within the chest. This is it! When we ask ourselves the question *How far will I go to help my neighbor?* we can remember Jesus and his definition that your neighbor is anyone who is in need.

When experiencing others who have a deep spiritual consciousness, some invisible but penetrating energy flows from one to the other. People feel better just sitting next to them. They are healing. There are really no words to adequately describe this type of experience. It is what happened at Gate 10 and it happens all over the world when unconditional love and selfless service are displayed.

Psychology has found that positive emotions such as joy and happiness widen our view of the world and expand our imaginations. When we feel positive, all things are possible. Happiness activates, makes exploration more likely, and is contagious.

I have found that if you can go through your life no matter what it throws at you, if in even the darkest of moments you can retain your faith of something greater than yourself, there is hope. If you are still able to laugh and see the beauty in yourself and others while stopping to play ball with the kids in the street, you can more than make it. When we become bitter and resentful, we continuously look for someone or something to blame. If we can stay out of these narcissistic, "poor little old me" traps and continue to find pleasure in the moment, the world opens itself up to us. Life is a splendid gift because of what it allows us to give to others.

Jesus displayed no trace of fear. He was not afraid of losing his reputation or even losing his life. He did nothing and compromised on nothing for the sake of even a modicum of prestige in the eyes of others. He did not seek anyone's approval. Jesus's courage, fearlessness, and independence made people ask, "Who is this man?"

What will people say of you? Are you willing to be anonymous? Anonymity was not designed for personal protection but as a way of viewing the world. Anonymity is real humility at work. It is giving up our natural egoic tendencies for the desire of personal distinction.

As the ego is deflated, the Self emerges. You cannot acquire it, pursue it, or get treated for it, as it was always there waiting for you to rediscover. As you work a spiritual program and move (transcend) from one level to the next, you move from lower energy levels of consciousness to higher levels of consciousness. Generally speaking, lower levels of consciousness are forms of negative energy, while the higher energy fields are positive energy. Lower levels of consciousness are correlated with the human attributes of desire, guilt, anger, fear, and resentment as persistent states of being. Our work in earlier chapters focused on getting beyond these lower levels of energy. Starting with this chapter, we concern ourselves with the positive energy states. As you reach the higher energy levels, acceptance, gratitude, love, and serenity become one's prevailing presence.

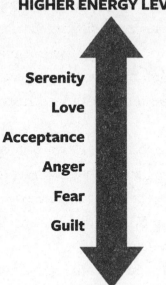

HIGHER ENERGY LEVELS

Serenity

Love

Acceptance

Anger

Fear

Guilt

LOWER ENERGY LEVELS

FIGURE 8.3. As one navigates the path of spiritual transformation, it is typical to move from negative energy states such as guilt and fear to higher energy states such as acceptance and love. Some people never experience this movement, others have dramatic spiritual experiences and dramatically move up the energy levels, and most will experience this over much time and effort through working a spiritual program.

So as the Self emerges, we see higher and higher levels of consciousness prevailing. Going back to the mountain metaphor, it makes sense that, as we climb higher and higher, everything becomes clearer. We can see farther, understand better, and are not limited to just a narrow view of what is happening around us. We can see the interrelatedness of things and how nothing really stands by itself. Everything is a part of something greater. Those at the bottom of the mountain see very little and lack an understanding of the interrelatedness of everything.

In Chapter 9, we will continue to explore the emerging Self. There are so many benefits to spiritual work, and in Chapter 9 I will try to describe more of them to you. By now I hope you don't need to be sold on the virtues of the Self. I believe you can grow spiritually by reading this book. If you spend time studying this book and some of the related references, you can dramatically change your life. These changes are not just exterior. Your whole essence, including your physiological self, will change remarkably for your and the world's betterment. By spiritual transformation, you make your life a gift to the world.

9

The Emergence of the Self

And I saw the river
over which every soul
must pass
to reach the kingdom
of heaven
and the name of that river
was suffering:
and I saw a boat
which carries souls
across the river
and the name of that boat
was love.

—Saint John of the Cross, 1542–91

When I was in a very bleak state at the start of my path toward enlightenment, I asked for God's help. I felt like a passenger on a ship going nowhere. Over time, when conditions were right, God granted my prayer. Then I asked God if I could come closer, and I continue to ask Him this question just about every day so that I can further understand what I can do to be the best servant and messenger I can possibly be. By God's grace, this journey has given me so much, and for that I am so grateful. Spiritual transformation has given me both joy and happiness. However, along the journey, I learned that even these things must be surrendered to move into a peace beyond all understanding. Now my life feels like it is being gently rocked by waves of love and peace.

Originally, I was motivated but confused. I was filled with energy, but had no clear path within which to channel it. I thought if I could spend time with spiritual people and read spiritual books, maybe by osmosis or diffusion it could become mine. I had difficulty finding a path that suited me. Ultimately, I chose the path of the mind, which seemed to make sense, considering the absolute credibility I had given to mental functioning. My life goal was to gain knowledge, and that had not necessarily changed, although now it was an entirely different type of knowledge—"knowingness"—I was after.

One path to liberation through the mind is Vedanta, an ancient Hindu path based on the following two simple propositions: (1) Human nature is divine, and (2) The aim of human life is to realize that human nature is divine. The goal of Vedanta is a state of self-realization achieved by the understanding that the Self or Atman is the same as God or Brahman. The Upanishadic quest is to understand Brahman, the source of everything, the Atman, the Self, and the relationship between Brahman and Atman. Thus, the path to liberation is through the mind, ridding oneself of all forms of thinking. This involves getting rid of or surrendering the motives, opinions, and character flaws of the ego. The motives and so on are the clouds in the sky, shielding us from our Self. To surrender everything to God does not leave you with "nothing," but leads to the awareness that one is "everything."

Our human mind is a reductionistic survival machine groomed to deal with the natural world of objects. It cannot grasp the "everything" or the infinite. Expecting the mind to understand infinity is akin to expecting a three-year-old to understand calculus. The only accurate description of the infinite is *neti*, meaning "not this . . . not this." If you were to travel the whole universe and beyond, saying to everything you can observe or conceive, "not this . . . not this," what remains would be God.

As you transcend the ego, you will experience the happiness and joy you were meant to enjoy. Most notably, when you reach the nonlinear realm of understanding, you will experience love as it is meant to be experienced: unconditionally. You might believe this is beyond you, but it is not.

Since nothing is caused by anything and everything happens when the conditions are right, there is no basis for blame. For example, you may pray to God for the ability to unconditionally love others. Instead, you might end up with a serious life problem to deal with. Instead of blaming God for your problems, you can see the opportunity to develop humility. This humility is necessary for you to be able to truly love others for what they are without trying to control or change them.

It is critical to remember that the more "knowingness" you have, the more God will expect from you. You will not be able to use the old rationalizations to determine that your behavior was somehow all right. If you want to move closer to God, you need to become His messenger on this earth. This is extremely demanding, but personally, I would have it no other way.

Finally, the constellation of the Self allows you to see the love and beauty inside even the most retched and downtrodden people. When this happens, you have become a healer and can reduce others' pain by the sheer energy of your presence. Such an example of the path of the heart is Mother Teresa. Mother Teresa was a Roman Catholic nun with Indian citizenship who founded the Missionaries of Charity in Calcutta in India in 1950. For more than forty-five years, she ministered to the poor, sick, orphaned, and dying while guiding the Missionaries of Charity's expansion, first throughout India and then in other countries. Mother Teresa's Missionaries of Charity continued to expand, and at the time of her death, it was operating 610 missions in 123 countries. With no concern for her own life or health, she loved those who were most unlovable to society, including those with leprosy.

As we view the world and our roles in it from the loftier perspective of the emerging Self, this clearer view allows for dramatic changes in knowledge, perception, and intention to take place. The physical brain actually changes, shifting from typically left dominant and analytical to right dominant and symbolic (see page 240).

The following occurs as part of the process of spiritual transformation:

- Access to greater knowledge
- Seeing the world differently
- Changing intention
- Love as unconditional love
- Changes in neurobiology

Access to Greater Knowledge

We acquire knowledge in many ways. In some instances, we are born with it. Our unconscious nervous system is hardwired with genetic knowledge regarding survival that is species specific. For example, if you give a small child black coffee without loading it with cream and sugar, she will spit it out. The reason for this is the fact that coffee is bitter. Most poisons are also bitter. At birth your body knows to reject anything unknown and bitter, as it may be harmful.

We unconsciously mediate social functioning. Interpreting facial expressions is genetically encoded. The fusiform facial area, part of the human visual system in the brain, helps determine identity and links faces to memory to tell us if it is a happy face and safe to approach or a negative, angry face signaling danger. We also have "Theory of Mind," which allows us to feel what others are feeling ("mirror neurons") and to come up with ideas about what the other might be thinking and considering.

Throughout life we learn through education and through information from friends, family, culture, and religion, and this information then becomes part of the separate self called the ego. "Knowingness" or knowledge from the field of consciousness is just another source of information, but there is one tremendous difference—it is truth without distortion.

Earlier we explored how the field of consciousness is a storehouse for everything happening in the past and present. We also learned that the field of consciousness only stores the truth. Consciousness, or the Holy Spirit, is the subjective, spiritual, unmanifest context behind everything created in our material world. So as you transcend to higher and higher levels of consciousness, you will be attracted to correspondingly higher fields of energy. These higher energy fields store knowledge applicable to that particular energy field. For example, five years ago Nancy was a bitter and depressed woman. She saw the world only as a source of depression and bitterness. The world was generally the same five years later, but due to her ongoing treatment and recovery, Nancy lived in what appears to her to be an entirely different world. This world is happier, lighter, and much friendlier. Her higher spiritual energy level influences her thoughts, feelings, and behavior. She does not associate with the people of five years ago. Nancy has greater knowledge and awareness, allowing her to make better choices for herself. She has achieved a greater "knowingness" because of her willingness to face herself and her fears.

As you pursue personal spiritual transformation, an unfolding, like that of a beautiful flower, takes place. This unfolding can be quick as a flash of light or slowly evolving like an orchid. Your resulting spiritual energy level is a great predictor of the kind of people you will be attracted to. When you are around someone with the same or very similar energy level, you sometimes feel like you can complete their sentences for them. You feel closeness and see "eye to eye" with this person. You often find you have similar worldviews and enjoy many of the same interests.

In modern physics, the term *attractor field* is a theoretical concept stating that based on one's level of spiritual consciousness, one is attracted to an attractor field of a similar energy level. Loosely translated, if the field of consciousness holds all truth, the more spiritual consciousness energy a person has the more truth he/she has access to. A positive attractor field is an energy force consisting of all the higher consciousness levels. Its qualities are openness, love, peace, acceptance, gratitude, forgiveness, serenity, nonjudgmentalism, and more. It feels good to be with or near someone whose energy radiates a positive attractor field. One becomes drawn in to the other's energy. Unfortunately, when you are no longer near a person with a higher level of consciousness, your level of consciousness tends to drop back to its normal level.

An *oppressor field* is the opposite. It pushes, forces, feels heavy, and is most definitely negative energy. The word "oppressor" comes from the Latin word *crusher* or *destroyer*. All lower levels of consciousness radiate this field to varying degrees. Righteousness, indignation, hate, jealousy, apathey, seduction, hopelessness, anger, grief, envy, pride, sabotage, cyncism, pity, discouragment, and indifference are just some of the qualities of these levels. A spiritual aspirant needs to avoid being around people who exude this negative field. It is best to keep such people at arm's length or eliminate them from your life. However, if such a person is in crisis and I believe I can help, I will move in closer as needed.

You might think it sounds harsh to eliminate certain people from your life; however, the greatest gift you give to the world is your own spiritual transformation, and if you are not single-minded in your journey, you will not get there. Emphasis on your spiritual growth is not selfish, for you are giving to the formation of the world. From this perspective, the choice is not hard to make.

In effect, consciousness is the record of everything that has happened since the birth of humankind up until this very moment. It does not contain the future, for the future is uncertain. The innovative biologist, Dr. Rupert Sheldrake, is the innovator behind the concepts of morphic fields and morphic resonance. This theory leads to an understanding of a living, developing universe with its own inherent memory (consciousness). Every human being draws upon and contributes to the collective memory of the species. This means that new patterns of behavior can spread more rapidly than would otherwise be possible. This theory and others like it hold that there is an intelligence formed by the history of the world and this intelligence is available as "knowingness." Greater "knowingness" is accessed by greater access to the field. Greater access is determined by one's spiritual growth, taking away the distortion of the ego and allowing the right hemisphere of the brain to communicate directly with the field.

Seeing the World Differently

When you erode the control of the ego, you start to see everything as an extension of the Self. There is no pathological attachment or nonattachment but a detachment from the emotional turmoil and an uncanny intuitive sense of life.

Please do not confuse the word "nonattached" with detachment. You become a part of the world but not of the world. Your concerns are for the welfare of humankind, since you live for the next world. Because of spiritual transformation, the world itself holds little attraction, as there is nothing that I want or need from it other than subsistence. It is the next world or life that holds an attraction, although I have no factual idea of what the mystery will be like.

Loss of ego allows you to view life from a reality-based and loving perspective. My great interest in life is to be of selfless service, which is all about helping the world. However, I am not distracted by emotion. This is especially true with negative emotions and their tendency to trigger old unconscious programs. It is not important how I or anyone feels about things; it is only important what I can do to be helpful.

You can sit around all day and talk about how horrible the world is, or you can ask yourself, "How can I be helpful?" Sometimes it is as simple as holding a door open for a mother holding a child or as complicated as a community project to reduce violence in the neighborhood. When you look for opportunities to help, they will present themselves. You might think of life as one karmic opportunity after another.

Early aspirants on the spiritual path often ask how they can help the world. Unfortunately, the egoic view of the world they inhabit is just an illusion. How do you fix an illusion? First work on yourself, and as you grow spiritually, you will answer your own question. Remember, you are connected to every-thing and everyone. As you grow, you take the world with you.

With each spiritual transformation, the ego is deflated and the truth about us becomes clearer. As the brain grows, the area allowing us to interact with the world in an adult fashion becomes more and more functional. As mentioned earlier, this area is referred to as the prefrontal cortex (PFC). The PFC is the seat of our conscience, allowing us to override primitive urges and impulses, and is where our executive functioning resides. Executive functioning includes the ability to abstract, conceptualize, solve new and novel problems, and perform tasks requiring advanced reasoning. The prefrontal cortex separates men and women from lower forms of animals. The PFC is a part of the "seeking system," and when this system is aroused by increasing the neurotransmitter dopamine, the PFC portion of the system looks for a "higher meaning" in life.

As we grow, our brains grow and become more complex. Complexity theory from nonlinear physics generally states that the more complex a system is, the more functional it is. The brain is very much this way, preferring to operate more dynamically with more neural connections. Early-life trauma and early-onset alcohol and drug use tend to diminish the age-appropriate complexity of the brain, creating many forms of difficulty, including changes in brain structure and function-ing. This can lead to problems in relationships called *attachment disorders*. Early experiences of relational trauma can lead to uncertainty about the self, as well as feelings of being unsafe and uncomfortable around others. This is an example of how the appearance of the world can change from a loving, caring place to one where no one or nothing can be trusted. It is easy to see from this how an unconscious program can come into being.

Give an eight-year-old a pre-algebra problem to solve. A young child's brain is usually not equipped to handle this level of complexity. However, give him/her the same problem at age twelve, and he/she can readily solve the problem now that the brain has the ability to abstract and conceptualize. When we were children, everything revolved around us. Years later, we may still manifest features of narcissism. Not very much has changed at all. The spiritual journey teaches us that the world is about "give and take" and not just "take." Later in the journey, we learn it is more important to give than to receive, and here is where the joy begins.

Life invites us to grow up. Sometimes the invitation is far from kind, as the bottom just drops out. Life lessons open our eyes, creating opportunities to gain knowledge. Think of your own life—full of ups and downs. If you have engaged a difficult, overwhelming situation in your life and walked through it, you have probably transcended to a greater understanding of yourself and the world you live in. For example, you lost a loved one you thought you could never live without. Utilizing the beatitude "Blessed are they who mourn, for they shall be comforted," we can see how love can be distorted by selfish desires to cling to the ephemeral. When we lose someone we love, it creates grief, but it also creates a spiritual opportunity to rise to a new level of freedom. We learn we can live without what we previously thought to be essential. We never lose anything that deserves to be loved; we just simply enter into a more mature relationship. Peace is the consolation.

Regardless of our personal shortcomings, when around others who always treat us with love and respect, we can learn to develop trust. Sometimes we did not trust the world and the world did not trust us. As we see others doing well in their spiritual journey, it allows us to develop realistic optimism and hope. Often the start of our spiritual journey was precipitated by a sense of hopelessness. An environment of hope and trust creates a brand-new way to perceive life. For many, there is a pull toward further growth and understanding. When this pull occurs, it is the Holy Spirit urging you onward to higher and higher levels of spiritual consciousness.

We learn we cannot do this alone. We learn that our ego doesn't have the answers. We learn to rely on something greater that ourselves and by doing so create an opportunity to "live" in the truest sense of the word.

Changing Intention

Strong intention is necessary to reach your spiritual goals. As you start to evolve spiritually, qualities such as love, forgiveness, patience, gratitude, and optimism will naturally grow within you. Love isn't something you can cultivate. You cannot find it in another or acquire it through psychotherapy. It is already inside of you. You cannot lose what you already have. Life cannot exist without the power of love. Life and love are one and the same.

One's intention shapes outcome. First of all, determine if the intention is egoic or Self in nature. In other words, am I striving for personal gain at another's expense, or is my intention altruistic? An example of Self-oriented intention is found in what can be described as the "divine paradox" of "giving it away to keep it." If I truly give of my true Self, my Self will be strengthened. When we genuinely give to others without looking for thanks, congratulations, or something in return, we establish a positive relationship with the field of consciousness such that what we get back is in multiples.

It is the change in intention from the "I," "me," and "mine" of the narcissistic ego to love emanating from the Self that serves as the basis for the joy of the spiritual journey. It takes a higher level of understanding to know from your own heart that what you give to the world comes back to you.

In the mid-1970s German physicist Fritz-Albert Popp discovered that all living things, from the simplest organism to the most complex human, emit a constant current of biophotons (light radiated from the cells). These light waves are an extremely effective communication system able to transfer information almost instantaneously. He discovered these tiny frequencies were emitted by the DNA in our cells, and the wavelength was rather stable, ranging from a few to several hundred photons per second per square centimeter of surface. However, when the organism was emotionally disturbed or suffered from a physical illness, the current went sharply up or down. For example, in cancer the frequency went down to a few photons, as if their light was going out. It could well be that there are energy frequencies that mediate healing. I believe this to be true, as the core of everything is energetic in composition.

Taking Popp's pioneering work further, Dr. Gary Schwartz was able to capture and record this light emanating from living things. He tested a number of healers and found a stream of light flowed from the healers' hands. Not only did healing intention cause waves of light, but these waves were among the most organized light waves found in nature. If thoughts are generated as wave frequencies, healing intention can be thought of as a well-ordered light. When intention is directed toward another or the world in general, it manifests as both electrical and magnetic energy and produces ordered streams of photons that are both visible and measurable.[55]

Intention is such an important consideration when looking at any thought or action. Your current state of mind has an effect on all life around you. Living things emit biophotons

---

[55] Lynne McTaggart, *The Intention Experiment* (New York: Free Press, 2007), 27–33.

that allow for communication, creating a highly sophisticated means of interaction. When you send an intention, it physically affects its recipient. Every major physiological system in your body is mirrored in the body of the receiver. When unconditional love is the intention, it creates the perfect manifestation of love—two bodies as one.[56]

Do you ever think about why someone contacts you just when you were thinking about them? Intention can increase or decrease biophoton emissions. Thoughts are just another stream of biophotons. Every thought augments or diminishes someone else's light. Neurophysiologist Jacobo Grinberg-Zylberbaum discovered that brain synchrony occurred among pairs of experimental participants separated by distance if they had a previous relationship.[57] Nonlinear physics calls this nonlocality. You do not have to be around someone to influence them. Once connected to someone, you are always connected.

Just think of this in terms of changing people, places, and things. Generally, we need to keep our distance from people who emit large amounts of negative energy. If you live or work around such people, take time to renew yourself. They can drain you of your energy, so spending time with other positive spiritual seekers in meditation, prayer, contemplation, or surrounded by beauty can help you recharge. By connecting only with those with positive intention of service work and by reciprocating with equal intention, we start to create our inner

---

[56] Ibid., 47.
[57] Ibid., 50.

and outer world. To save the world, we must first save ourselves and become instruments of peace and love.

As you grow in spiritual wisdom, your intention will change.
My sense of intention became exclusively to perform every
action with love and integrity and not be attached to the outcome. I learned years ago when you teach and your teachings are
about God, Jesus, and the Holy Spirit, there will always be people who put you down and take shots at you. I hear things like,
"The state shouldn't pay him because he talked about Jesus," or
"I didn't come here to hear a sermon," or "Dr. Nuckols should
stick with neurobiology and get away from nonscientific stuff,"
and "I used to love his presentations, but I don't need spiritual
teaching to help my clients." Years ago I was so self-critical and
perfectionistic that these kinds of evaluations would keep me
up all night. Now I try to remember that people are perfect and
just where they need to be on their own journeys. They are just
not ready for what I had to say at that time, or as an atheist or
agnostic, the words may have little meaning to them. I also try to
understand the many different avenues there are to Self; individuals need to find their own paths.

The African word *ubuntu* gives us another wonderful way to
think about intention. *Ubuntu* is a central tenet of philosophy
that addresses what it means to be human. The word is defined
in two parts. The first part speaks of genuineness toward other
human beings. This involves being hospitable, generous, compassionate, and caring. People with *ubuntu* are said to be

welcoming and kindly in their attitude. The second aspect of *ubuntu* concerns the sharing of personal worth and, in doing so, becoming inextricably bound to others. The bottom line is that the only way we can be human is by being together.

Prayer of St. Francis of Assisi

Lord, make me an instrument of thy peace.

Where there is hatred, let me sow love.

Where there is injury, pardon.

Where there is doubt, faith.

Where there is despair, hope.

Where there is darkness, light.

Where there is sadness, joy.

O Divine Master, grant that I may not

so much seek to be consoled as to console;

to be understood as to understand;

to be loved, as to love.

For it is in giving that we receive.

It is in pardoning that we are pardoned.

It is in dying to self that we are born to eternal life.[58]

---

[58] http://www.thesacredheart.com/pfran.htm.

Love—Unconditional Love

What an incredible journey life is. Like the transformation of a caterpillar to a butterfly, the original object was certainly not very lovely to look at and sometimes even tougher to be around. It seemed in the past many of us were at odds with the world. Now, by way of a spiritual transformation, we are different people, in tune with the world.

> *Just as you want men to do to you, do to them likewise. For if you love those who love you, what is your blessing? For even sinners love those who love them. And if you do good only to those who do good to you, what is your blessing? For sinners also do the same.*
>
> *And if you lend only to him for whom you expect to be paid back, what is your blessing? For sinners also lend to sinners, to be paid back likewise. But love your neighbors and do good to them, and lend and do not cut off any man's hope; so your reward will increase and you will become sons of the Highest; for he is gracious to the wicked and the cruel. Be therefore merciful, as your Father is also merciful.*[59]

When I speak of *love,* I mean unconditional love. It is the kind that you cannot buy. Most of us have been raised on conditional love, which is not even love at all. Probably some have been raised where there was no or little of any kind of apparent

---

[59] Luke 6: 31–36, *Holy Bible,* trans. George M. Lamsa.

love from parents and caregivers. All of us want and require love. We think about it, fantasize about it, and go to great lengths to achieve it. We feel that our lives are incomplete without it. It is a source of great fantasy and confusion.

Our misconceptions about love started when we were very young. When you or I did all the right things—we were clean, ate our broccoli, got good grades, and remained quiet while in the house—people loved us. They smiled and spoke to us lovingly. But when we got into a fight, flunked a test, forgot to take out the garbage or make up our bed, we were deemed bad. This kind of love is based on conditions. *If you do this I will love you, but if you don't do what I want you to do, I will not love you.* When we grow up like this it is very difficult to discover who we are because we are too busy trying to please others. Unconscious programs for happiness can grow in such an environment. We might have problems with affection and esteem or grow up trying to control everything so we will be loved. Unfortunately such programs only cause us misery. It is only in an environment of unconditional love that the child is free to explore and learn.

We can understand other ways this leads to the ego's unconscious programs for happiness. For example, as a child you might have been told not to hang around with a certain type of person. Maybe it was because of their race or socioeconomic status. We call this prejudice. But as a child we had to follow these so-called rules that were designed to be for our protection (actually due to a multigenerational pattern of hate). When we act just to get the approval of others by what we say and do, we are paying for the attention we should be given freely, and we will not feel genuinely loving or loved in this way.

It is only unconditional love that can fill us up, make us whole, and ultimately lead us to the happiness we all desire. This is the kind of love—one for another—that caused those fifteen people to meet at Gate 10; it is the kind of love that reaches out to anyone in need. This is the kind of love that has no limits or expectations. It is going out at midnight to help another in need. It is being a good neighbor. It is expecting nothing in return. Love cares for the happiness of another person without expecting anything in return. This kind of love never runs out of energy and gets stronger the more it is given away.

When you can surround yourself with people who are all right with you even when you make foolish mistakes, when you fail to do what they want, when things don't turn out so well and throughout all of this they love you and support you, what a wonderful place to grow into yourself. Most people spend their entire lives trying to fill the emptiness inside of themselves, trying to find love.

God is love and the Self inside of you is love. Love brings happiness and joy. Life is a spiritual journey to God's love, a love that resonates with our fellows and with the God of our

understanding, and is present and available to those who suffer, no questions asked and no price to pay.

One of the most difficult aspects to love is that we must first
love ourselves before we can genuinely love another. Love can
only be kept by being given away. True happiness is found in
unselfish love. It must be shared freely and accepted freely.
Love prefers the good of another to my own but it does not
even compare the two. How can it, as we are all one. Love concerns itself only with seeking the good for one who is loved.
Therefore, love is its own reward. As I send love out into the
world, the world sends it right back to me.

To truly love we must first love truth. This truth is God
Himself living in my brothers and sisters. If I am selfish with
love, I do not respect the rights of others. If I withhold love as
a condition of compliance, the relationship will not grow. I
must grant the other person room to grow instead of trying to
control that person with conditional love. Selfish love is
tricky. It tends to appear unselfish by making concessions to
the other in order to control them. Love does not make limited
concessions. It is whole and forthcoming, with no small print
at the bottom. Our destiny is to love one another as Christ
loved us.

There is a certain truth to compassion. To feel for someone
from our hearts is to feel intimately. Unconditional love has
the element of compassion in that the experience of compassion is the experience of feeling and/or suffering with another.

To suffer or to feel with humanity is to be in tune with and experience the impulses and rhythms of life. It makes one authentic and truly at one with the all. Compassion and love are congruent with the flow of consciousness as ultimate consciousness (Holy Spirit) is the energy of God's love.

At extremely low levels of spiritual energy, love is a biological process called lust. As we move higher up into the areas of reason, we try to analyze—in a reductionist fashion—what this thing called love is really all about. The ego sees love as an opportunity to possess and control. When we reach the nonlinear realms, we understand love holistically. It is a way of being in the world that genuinely comes from the heart. It accepts all without judgment.

As one goes through a personal spiritual transformation and reaches a loftier perch on the mountainside, the difference in spiritual consciousness between, for example, a husband and wife might become vastly greater than before. This can lead to some initial problems but may also inspire the spouse to move forward in her/his own spiritual journey. Again, we can see this problem from the perspective of a spiritual opportunity. Just being around someone with a higher level of spiritual energy can be helpful because of the pervasiveness of the energy. Spiritual energy through love is always looking to find ways to better the world. As Dr. David Hawkins states, "Acceleration of spiritual energy is facilitated by the relinquishment of narcissistic, egotistic self-interests, such as the seeking of personal gain. The energy is facilitated by the intention and alignment of humility, mercy, compassion, and dedication to the relief of suffering of others in the forms of benevolence, mercy and kindness."[60]

We can say that love is an energy force that connects us to everything in the universe. It is an unconditional state that characterizes human nature. It is knowledge that is always there for us if we can learn to open ourselves up to it. I truly believe that it is the emptying out of all that we are that allows for the Holy Spirit to fill us up. The more we empty ourselves out the more room there is for God's love. Think of the whole process described in this book as an emptying out of all of our old illusions. The more we clean out, the more we gain. What a lovely exchange; the misery and suffering of the ego for the love of God.

Love emanates from the Self but desire emanates from the ego. At this point in the journey, the difficult task is to let go of judgmentalism and other forms of reductionist thinking and move into Love as a way of being in the world. There really are no words to describe the essence of who you are. God's love just is. When we love, we are expressing our essence and the essence of God. There is no opposite of love.

Unconditional love is the goal of most spiritual aspirants. I once had a minister tell me that he did not feel anyone could achieve this level of spiritual evolution in the human form. He

---

[60] Hawkins, *Transcending the Levels of Consciousness*, 258.

said, "I don't even try because it puts too much pressure on me." Actually, I have found that when you are "called," you are pulled from the future and the effort is "effortless," so to speak. Up until this point, it is a lot of hard work and single-mindedness of effort, but once you start being pulled from the future, you cannot spend enough time in spiritual study as it becomes joyful. At least this was my experience. Not to believe in the inevitability of unconditional love is to deny the presence of the Self. I feel love from everything.

Changes in Our Neurobiology

You are no doubt familiar with illustrations of the two distinct hemispheres of the brain. Interestingly, these two sides are connected by only 300 million axonal fibers running from one hemisphere to the other. Both the left and right hemispheres are interested in different things, but together they work to insure our well-being and allow us to function in the world. Everything we experience is processed in the brain, but how much can we trust what our brain perceives? Consider this excerpt from *Scientific American Mind*:

> *It is a fact of neuroscience that everything we experience is actually a figment of our imagination. Although our sensations feel accurate and truthful, they do not necessarily reproduce the physical reality of the outside world. Of course, many experiences in daily life reflect the physical stimuli that enter the brain. But the same neural machinery that interprets*

actual sensory inputs is also responsible for our dreams, delu-
sions and failings of memory. In other words, the real and the
imagined share a physical source in the brain. So take a lesson
from Socrates: "All I know is that I know nothing."[61]

To understand left and right hemispheric functioning, let's start with an appreciation of the moment and then expand our knowledge from there. The right side of the brain works in silence using symbols. It is holistic, spontaneous, and empathic and likes being in the moment. This hemisphere takes the sensory (both external and internal) input and constructs a "collage" of the moment. It tells us what the moment feels like, tastes like, smells like, looks like, and sounds like. The right hemisphere processes only what it receives and nothing more.

As Jill Bolte Taylor describes in her book *My Stroke of Insight*,[62] this hemisphere connects us to all of the energy around us. We are all just energy beings connected to everything around us through the consciousness of our right hemisphere. While in the right hemisphere, we can feel serenity within ourselves with no external requirement for happiness, and without being caught up in the past and future. When we are in our right hemisphere ("right mind"), we are in touch with the consciousness of the field. The right hemisphere seems to be attached to the

---

[61] Stephen L. Macknik and Susan Martinez-Conde, *Scientific American Mind*, October/November 2008, 20.
[62] Jill Bolte Taylor, *My Stroke of Insight*.

"oneness" of everything and every action.

On the other hand, the egoic left hemisphere is more concerned with the past and future and is interpretative. The left hemisphere takes this "collage" of the moment and looks at it from a logical, literal, and verbal perspective. It takes what information it has and comes up with a story to explain the information within the context of our lives.

This hemisphere looks for closure and has an "interpreter" function that fills in the blanks to tell a cohesive story. In other words, the left hemisphere takes the part of the story it is given and fills in the empty spaces to develop a coherent presentation. This function has been described as the left hemisphere interpreter.[63] The left hemisphere tends to elaborate and make inferences about the material presented, often at the expense of veracity.[64] This hemisphere assigns meaning even when none is present. This is why ten people can observe the same scene and all describe it differently.

The left hemisphere thinks in language. It is the ongoing "chatter" in our heads that we cannot control. The left hemisphere is calculating intelligence involved in survival and personal gain. It is a separate self and says, "I am." This separates us from everything and everyone else on this planet.

---

[63] David J. Turk, Todd F. Heatherton, C. Neil McRae, William M. Kelley, and Michael S. Gazzaniga. "Out of Contact, Out of Mind: The Distributed Nature of Self," *Annals of the New York Academy of Sciences* 1001, no. 65 (2003).

[64] Janet Metcalfe, Margaret Funnell, and Michael S. Gazzaniga, "Right Hemisphere Memory Superiority: Studies of a Split-Brain Patient," *Psychological Science* 6 (3): 157–64.

Think of this in terms of the workings of your own mind. The left hemisphere, with its fear-driven concern for the past and future, is essentially what I am describing as the ego. It is the part of our sophisticated brain that makes us a smart but selfish animal.

The right hemisphere allows us to lose all of the complications of the past and future. In this hemisphere, we remain in the moment, allowing for connection with the highest consciousness or the Holy Spirit and feelings of happiness and joy. It is this hemisphere that allows us to connect with other humans in a healing way. One unconscious mind can communicate with another unconscious mind to create a therapeutic (helping or healing) alliance or bond, which is the core of the change mechanism. While the left hemisphere attends to talking and overt communication, the right hemisphere concerns itself with bonding and attachment in a healing alliance, especially if the mother, father, clinician, or teacher has come to appreciate the power of the Self. I call this "resonance." When we truly connect—resonate—with another, healing and growth take place.

Throughout this book, we have been working on deflating the ego and defining the Self. While this is taking place, the brain moves from left-dominant (language-dominant) to right-brain dominant. While left-brain dominant, negative stimuli can produce a strong fear reaction by swiftly triggering the amygdala (emotional memory) to respond. This sends the individual into a "fight-or-flight" or "freeze" survival midbrain response.

As one moves more into the right hemisphere, the reaction is stronger and faster to the prefrontal areas, allowing reason to prevail instead of a survival response. After climbing well up the mountain, you will develop an etheric or energy brain that is extremely intuitive. Intuitive awareness is what I have been referring to as "knowingness." From this perspective, one can see everything for what it is without being overwhelmed by a strong emotional response.

There are a vast number of ways to increase our contact with consciousness through our right hemispheres. Along with deflating the ego, I have found it very beneficial to develop my right hemisphere. As a left-brain scientist taught to analyze everything, this was not easy for me. The result has been a profound appreciation for beauty in all forms and the ability to see the beauty in all things.

Some of the techniques and strategies I have used to nurture my right hemisphere include aromatherapy (I like essential oils of clove, almond, and vanilla); listening to soothing music (I like Gregorian chants, classical music, and Native American drum and flute, among others); meditation (I prefer centering prayer, see page 252); eating tryptophan-rich (or calming) foods (such as eggs, cheese, and soy products) and avoiding sugary (hyper-inducing) foods; caring for my skin with massage and bathing; and surrounding myself with beautiful things, such as pictures of loved ones, inspirational sayings, flowers, or symbols of love and beauty. Also, you may want to try looking at things with "spiritual vision." Take in a landscape, but rather than focusing on the details with your left brain, see "past" the details with your right brain, as if you are looking at the scene with your peripheral vision. I hope some of these ideas are helpful to you. By the way, be thoughtful of others' dislikes and likes when adding sounds and scents to a common living area.

Be careful to avoid too much negative energy. Pay attention to how people, places, and things feel to you. This is a variation of "stick with the winners" or stay with "holy company." I have found certain people in my life who have not wanted to change but seemed to always try to bring me down to a lower egoic level, leaving me feeling confused and a little disoriented after they leave. Sometimes I have to put distance between those kinds of people and myself. However, in their time of need, I will respond to the call.

When you are in the right hemisphere, everything is silent and peaceful. This is where you go during a walk in nature, strolling through the woods or on a beach at sunset. This is where beauty takes you—a beautiful painting or piece of music. Mindfulness meditation and centering prayer strive to create this feeling state outside of space and time. These are the times in your life—looking into your newborn's face or your lover's eyes—when there is nothing but the two of you as "one" and time stands still. Being able to spend time in the right hemisphere is very good for your mental health. During the spiritual journey, the brain actually starts operating more from the right side, giving you a more holistic and integrated perspective of the world. The right brain sees everything as "one" and everyone as intimately connected to everyone and everything.

I pray that these last chapters have helped you along your personal path whatever it might be leading you. Take care of yourself, for you are the world. Do not depend on others to make things all right for you. Take the time to nurture yourself, and it becomes easy to nurture those around you. In fact, your very presence will nurture your family, coworkers, community, and the world.

Everything leads us back toward the "Light." We are all on the journey home. As Elisabeth Kübler-Ross so beautifully states, "When we have passed the tests we are sent to Earth to learn, we are allowed to graduate. We are allowed to shed our body, which imprisons our souls."

10

Being One with Everything

There is a river flowing now very fast. It is so great and swift that there are those who will be afraid. They will try to hold on to the shore. They will feel they are being torn apart, and they will suffer greatly. Know the river has its destination. The elders say we must let go of the shore, push off into the middle of the river, keep our eyes open, and our heads above the water. See who is in there with you and celebrate.

At this time in history, we are to take nothing personally. Least of all, ourselves. For the moment that we do, our spiritual growth and journey comes to a halt. The time of the lone wolf is over. Gather yourselves! Banish the word struggle from your attitude and your vocabulary. All that we do now must be done in a sacred manner and in celebration. We are the ones we've been waiting for.

—The Elders, Oraibi, Arizona Hopi Nation

Yes, I believe we are the ones. The elders are correct. There is no time to hesitate, and the road is narrow. The time to work on your spiritual destiny is now. There has never been a time when so much spiritual information is available. For me, faith changed my course in life and created a willingness and longing to become intimate with God. Faith was the gift I was given. Faith is a surrendering of will—not my will, but *Thy will be done.*

The journey is an uphill climb until you arrive home and into God's arms. Intellectual concepts and dogma cannot get you there. The climb is painful at times and joyful at others. You will constantly bump up against your own worst fears. Open up to the Holy Spirit, who works on our spiritual evolution, not only by purifying us from within but also by the life challenges and difficulties from without. *Everything is part of the journey.*

This lifetime can be described using the words of the Grateful Dead: "What a long, strange trip it's been," coming out of purgatory to a life where simply being alive is joyful. We have totally reversed our role in life from "taker" to "giver." We have learned to care for others not because of what they could do for us, but because of what we might be able to do for them. We have learned that giving is receiving and we are all "one," moving in some strange dance across time. Where you will arrive at spiritually is hard to determine. It is an individual matter between you and God. However, you will be much more spiritually in tune with the world if you devote your life to spiritual understanding and transformation.

The journey is about discovering the truth in ourselves and others. It is learning to be all right with what we humbly are. Truth is "One," but expressions of truth are limitless. Throughout the journey, we have learned that truth is simple and apparent once it is rediscovered. It comes from the heart, not the head. The wonderful outcome of spiritual transformation includes:

- Being able to look at ourselves and others with a much greater degree of compassion;
- Not being compelled or controlled by the security, affection, power, control, and survival needs of the ego;
- Being able to love without conditions;
- Being able to detach from the emotionality of the world and to see things as they really are;
- Being content in our aloneness, often preferring calm and silence to the noise of the world we used to hide in;
- Being able to help others due to the healing energy of the Self;
- Being capable of rigorous self-honesty.

There are other spiritual tasks to learn and accomplish when we seek higher levels of spiritual consciousness. These include:

- The ability to totally accept everything just the way it is without desire to control or manipulate;
- The ability to be genuinely nonjudgmental and totally forgiving;
- The ability to reach a point of detachment from the

world—to be in this world but not part of the petty, egoic, day-to-day struggles.

Once Again, Surrendering the Ego's Unconscious Programs for Happiness

Go back and review Chapter 7 for a moment. That chapter discussed three steps for letting go of the ego's unconscious programs for happiness, which have been causing you so much misery and suffering. Those steps are:

Step 1: Affirmation of basic goodness (Self);

Step 2: Becoming aware over time of whatever in us is opposed to the image in Step 1;

Step 3: Dismantling the emotional programs of the ego—healing the problem and not just managing the symptoms.

Continually working on these three steps and eliminating the secondary gain of the ego is critically important for spiritual transformation. As you vertically dwell down into the defects of character and surrender them one by one to God, the Self shines through. The ego's unconscious programs for happiness are exposed and no longer influence your thinking, feeling, or behavior. Total deflation of the ego allows for the emergence of pure Self.

Remember, the ego is not bad, but it is the source of all suffering. The origin of the ego is the Self, and now it is on its journey to its home. The Self reabsorbs the ego, so to speak. While this egoless state is the prerequisite for enlightenment, enlightenment can occur only with Divine assistance.

These three steps help us get rid of much of the force of the ego, but when using a contemplative approach, there are several more steps. These steps, as described by Saint John of the Cross—a Spanish mystic, Carmelite friar and priest, and major figure of the Catholic Reformation—highlight the struggle the spiritual aspirant generally goes through late in the spiritual journey.

Step 4: The Night of Sense

In Step 4 there is an intuitive awareness of the facts that *one cannot find happiness in the gratification of the ego's programs for happiness* and *one cannot find happiness through the symbols we use for achieving a sense of security and survival, affection and esteem, and power and control.*

There is an upside and a downside to this conscious awareness. On one side, you are now in a place of internal freedom for the first time since you were a small child. You have now created the space for the Holy Spirit to do its work. However, you have been living under the delusions of the ego for so long that there may be disillusionment, discouragement, or even some degree of depression. This is to be expected, as any radical change can precipitate a process of grief. Perhaps when feeling empty, alone, or even abandoned, it is possible to feel like God is not there for you. God is always there for you. This is only a projection of unresolved grief or belief that God is displeased with you. Also, do not be saddened for not living up to the impossible expectations of the idealized image you had of yourself. Do not dwell on the past and how things should have been or could have been if only the cards were dealt differently. Doing this is an ego trip. Be patient as you continue to single-mindedly engage in your spiritual pursuits.

Step 5: The Night of Spirit

When liberated from most attachments and freedom has been attained, the freedom *from something* must now change to a freedom *for something*. In the spiritual life, it is love, which allows us to fulfill the two great commandments: to love God and to love others. Sometimes, it may feel like you are working so hard on your spiritual program but nothing is happening. This can lead to frustration. This is not uncommon. There may be relatively long dry periods, and then all of a sudden, a leap of spiritual growth takes place. Remember, everything happens when the conditions align for it to happen. These difficult periods can still be very productive and lead to a deepening relationship with God. This is when our persistence and dedication are tested.

The ability to delay gratification with discipline and dedication is critical. We must be able to hold desires in abeyance and

surrender our personal will to God at every moment. Ultimately, everything must be surrendered to God. Therefore,
each thought, desire, feeling, craving, and impulse is surrendered to God. As you do this, you will find your mind becoming increasingly quiet. The movement into the serenity of the
right hemisphere is taking place. You will suddenly understand that there is no "in here" and no "out there," as everything seamlessly merges into one. As this happens, you will
appreciate unconditional love.

When the understanding that you are one with everything
moves and settles into your heart, you have achieved the nonlinear realm. You are now radiating love from the heart and
bypassing much of the analytical left hemisphere. This is one of
the most joyous times along the journey; you will see love and
beauty in everything. The world is vibrantly alive. The joy you
can experience in the simplest of things is incredible. I recall
sitting in a Japanese garden on the campus of Furman
University watching the motion of the water in a small creek and
the dance of the algae as the stream caused a most incredible
waltz to manifest. My whole body shivered in delight. This was
but one beautifully joyful moment along my spiritual journey.

When the ego returns to the Self, which is its true origin,
there is an incredible sense of returning "home." You have a
sense of complete and utter silence, peace, and absence of fear
and suffering, and the realization that death and the sense of a
separate self are just an illusion. The body ultimately returns

to its origin—dust to dust—but the Self goes on forever and is truly one with all creation. Deeply understanding our union with all living things creates a sense of seamless connection within. Even in our aloneness, we feel aligned with everything and everyone.

In the gospel of John, Jesus delivered the following blessing, which speaks directly to this nonlinear unity: "So that they all may be one; just as thou, my father, art with me, and I am with thee, that they also may be one with us: so that the world may believe that thou didst send me. And the glory which thou gavest me, I gave to them; so that they may be one just as we are one. I with them and thou with me, that they may become perfected in one; so that the world may know that thou didst send me, and that thou didst love them just as thou didst love me."[65]

The Top of the Mountain

As I have indicated, there are levels of spiritual consciousness even beyond that of unconditional love. Who can tell if one has reached the top of the mountain? Only those who have been there, and even then, they can only tell you what the top of the mountain looked like to them. However, the experience of enlightenment has been described in very similar ways by those who have reached for it, and have the grace of God to thank for the experience. For thousands of years, in all areas of

---

[65] John 18:21–23, *Holy Bible,* trans. George M. Lamsa.

the world, and among all cultures, the experience has been described in very similar fashion. It is the Self returning Home to its maker. It is the Light returning to the Light. It is outside of the linear, material paradigm we live in, and our language fails to grasp the experience.

One of the great problems in understanding the nonlinear world of the unmanifest is that our English language deals with concepts and interactions between unmoving objects, and because of this, the quantum world is removed from us by the nature of our language. Our language works in terms of nouns and verbs, so we see only objects and their interactions, as well as concepts and categories, which causes a rigidity of thought. The nonlinear world flows and everything is connected, giving a category of "one." How can the ego compare and contrast "one"? In all honesty, the experience of the nonlinear, subjective spiritual state is ineffable, but I still try to explain it.

In the foreword to the book *Halfway Up the Mountain*, Mariana Caplan states:

What is enlightenment? Is it a continuous state of freedom and bliss, as most of us, at one time or another, have fantasized it to be? Does it bring an end to suffering, as we would like to hope? Is it an abiding non-dual context from which one can function with great skill and compassion, engaged in the manifest world of reality, while remaining anchored somehow in the formless Absolute? Or is it simply the capacity to awaken again and again, moment to moment, and actually be with

*what is? Although certainly representing one of the enlight-
ened traditions, my own teacher, Chogya Trungpa Rinpoche,
much preferred to talk about being awake, about being on the
spot, about cultivating wakefulness and compassion in the
midst of all our pain and confusion.*[66]

Enlightenment is really about an awakening. Becoming
enlightened doesn't make a person better than those who have
not experienced it. If anything, it allows the enlightened to
understand equality among us at greater depth. It is about
being in the moment and about seeing the essence in things
without being encumbered by all of the abstractions. It is
about unconditional love and how one can serve the world. It
is about being close to everything.

Most of the time, I feel little or no separation from anyone
and anything around me. It is about resting in the infinite
silence of God. It is about everything and nothing. It is not
about feeling good all the time. My arthritic body can tell you
that. Sometimes, I intensely feel the feelings of others, even if
they are negative. To see things as they really are without having ego defenses can be painful. It is certainly not about the
New Age fantasy of love, bliss, and peace without exception.

As a gift from God, it is not about an experience you can
own. To me, it is about being content wherever I am and doing
whatever I am called to do in the moment. It is a sense of calm-

---

[66] Mariana Caplan, *Halfway Up the Mountain* (Prescott, AZ: Hohm Press, 2001),
xiii.

ness and contentment and of eternal thanks. It is certainly about reveling in all of the beauty that is everywhere around me, beauty that was always there but that I could never see and appreciate before. I have come to appreciate a peace beyond all understanding. There is neither need nor desire for anything. Existence is complete just as it is. All life moves from complete to complete.

Many people have experiences that take them "out of this world," so to speak. For example, Bill Wilson, the cofounder of Alcoholics Anonymous, had a white-light experience that took him into the nonlinear realm of existence. In December 1934, he was in Towns Hospital in New York, once more trying to free himself from the demon alcohol. A friend, Ebby, who had recently found recovery through the Oxford Group, a Christian movement with a strong following in Europe and America in the 1920s and '30s stopped by. Bill asked him for the formula, and Ebby shared his experience. Sitting in the hospital room by himself, Bill related the intensity of the experience:

> *Lying there in conflict, I dropped in to the blackest depression I have ever known. Momentarily my prideful depression was crushed. I cried out, "Now I am ready to do anything— anything to receive what my friend Ebby has." Though I certainly didn't expect anything, I did make this frantic appeal, "If there is a God, will He show Himself!" The result was instant, electric beyond description. The place seemed to light up, blinding white. I knew only ecstasy and seemed on a mountain. A great wind blew, enveloping and penetrating me. To*

me, it was not of air but of Spirit. Blazing, there came the
tremendous thought, "you are a free man." Then the ecstasy
subsided. Still on the bed, I now found myself in a new world of
consciousness which was suffused by a Presence. One with the
Universe, a great peace came over me. I thought, "So this is the
God of the preachers, this is the great Reality." But soon my so-
called reason returned, my modern education took over and I
thought I must be crazy and I became terribly frightened.[67]

There are other contemporary descriptions of what happens
during the experience of enlightenment. Dr. David Hawkins
chronicles his experience in detail in his books. In the "About
the Author" section in his book *Reality, Spirituality and Modern
Man,* he says, "Suddenly, without warning, a shift in awareness
occurred and the Presence was there, unmistakable and all
encompassing. There were a few moments of apprehension as
the self died, and then the absoluteness of the Presence
inspired a flash of awe. This breakthrough was spectacular,
more intense than anything before. It has no counterpart in
ordinary experience. The profound shock was cushioned by
the love that is with the Presence. Without the support and
protection of that love, one would be annihilated."[68]

His journey went deep into the spiritual realm where he had
to address the "void." In the "void," he was offered all power.
He possessed a knowingness that allowed him to refuse. The
void is infinitely beautiful, but lacks one thing: the love of God.

---

[67] http://serentiyfound.org/history/billwspiritual.html
[68] David Hawkins, *Reality, Spirituality and Modern Man* (Toronto: Axial, 2008), 444

In my own experience, a sense of pervasive evil existed when I was in the "void."

The following is an experience described by Elizabeth Kübler-Ross:

It became for the first time in my life, an issue of faith. And the faith had something to do with a deep, inner knowledge that I had the strength and the courage to endure this agony by myself. But it also included the faith and the knowledge that we are never given more that we can bear. I suddenly became aware that all I needed to do was to stop my fight, to stop my rebellion, to stop being a warrior and move from rebellion to a simple, peaceful positive submission—to an ability to simply say "yes" to it.... Once I did that, the agony stopped and my breathing was easier. My physical pain disappeared at the moment I uttered the word "yes," not in words but in thoughts. And instead of the thousand deaths, I lived though a rebirth beyond human description.... It started with a very fast vibration, or pulsation, of my abdominal area which spread through my entire body and then to anything my eyes could see—the ceiling, the wall, the floors, the furniture, the bed, the window, the horizons outside of my window, the trees, and eventually the whole planet earth. It was as if the whole planet was in a very high speed vibration, every molecule vibrated. At the same time, something that looked like a lotus flower bud appeared and opened into an incredible, beautiful, colorful flower. Behind the lotus flower appeared the light that my patients so often talk about. And as I approached this light through the open lotus flower, with a whirl in a deep, fast vibration, I gradually and slowly merged into this incredible unconditional love, into this light. I became one with it."[69]

---

[69] Kübler-Ross, *On Life After Death*, 66–67.

Hundreds of thousands have had near-death experiences (NDEs). After the experience, they often come back with a higher level of spiritual consciousness. A near-death experience refers to a broad range of personal events associated with impending death. The experiencer can encounter multiple sensations, including detachment from the body; feelings of levitation; total serenity, security, or warmth; the experience of absolute dissolution; and the presence of a light, which some people interpret as a deity. Some see NDEs as a paranormal and spiritual glimpse into the afterlife. For some, the occurrence creates extreme fear. The following is an example of a firsthand report of an NDE:

It was a suicide attempt in 1986. I was asphyxiating on CO_2. I drifted up and into a long tunnel. At first, I felt pain and sorrow. I felt, from the perspective of all those affected by me, any hurt I had caused them. It was horrible but I was forced to understand my negative influence on them. It was incredibly enlightening. I would call it purgatory and I'm glad I didn't have to stay long! Then I floated along some more. The tunnel walls seemed to be made up of moving images. I was floating as in a warm salt bath and I was very comfortable. I found I could think clearly with no distractions. There was no music in my head as there usually was. A calming voice told me that everything would be explained when I arrived. I trusted this voice.

Arriving at the end of the tunnel I was greeted by a man who looks pretty much like I do today. He brought me to the edge of whatever I was standing on and when I looked into the inky blackness, all sense of time vanished. There was no past, present or future. Only everything all at once. I felt a tremendous understanding of the nature of the universe and my place in it. He showed me what looked like a huge white obelisk floating in the blackness. As I looked at it more closely, I saw that the surface was moving. It was a giant puzzle and it looked like it was being solved. He showed me my place and how the puzzle was re-arranged with each action by anyone on earth. Some of the puzzle had already fallen into place and I knew that something wonderful was going to happen when it was complete. Of course, I don't remember what it is but I still look forward to it! I was then sent back to my body. I didn't want to go and I fought it. I was angry for about two weeks to have had such utter peace taken from me.[70]

True enlightenment involves not only the very beautiful and dramatic experience that Bill and others describe, but the enlightened stay at a very high state of spiritual transformation; they do not come back. One of the great differences is in the workings of the ego. When you have an experience like Bill's or the experience of an NDE and come back, the ego still remains. It appears that Bill's ego was still engaged up to his departure from this world. When you cross over and the Self absorbs the ego, your brain exists in a state of total silence. There is no more left-hemisphere egoic "chatter" that is constantly telling you what to do.

I read about many individuals claiming to be in an enlightened

---

[70] http://www.mindspring.com/~scottr/nde/puppet.html.

state. Unfortunately, their egos give them away. Still full of judgmentalism and anger, they seem to find everything wrong with existence but fail to see the perfection and beauty. When there is no more ego, motives, judgments, and opinions cease, and only the absolute truth becomes important. Often telling this truth via "knowingness" is perceived by others in a negative way as it attracts egoic perception and negative judgment: "Who do you think you are?" When in an enlightened state, the Self knows, and you intuitively let it guide you.

God's Call

Everyone is called by God to reach the fullest potential of the Self. This is the core spiritual and fundamental Self. Because of it, there is a yearning for eternity that stretches beyond the confines of our countless self-expressions. Saying yes to this yearning and opening one's heart and mind to the mystery is the foundation of all spiritual life.

Through the Self, God continually communicates to us in love—the true form He wants our lives to take. Much of this communication involves being in circumstances where we are given the opportunity to overcome obstacles and test our faith. Judgment day is every moment of every day of your life. There will be many choices and occasions from which to learn. Always think and act wisely from the intention of love and integrity. God waits with infinite gentleness and patience for our response to His invitations.

The mystery of your deepest Self cannot be measured with a Rorschach test; nor can it be seen on an MRI. You will not always be able to defend your beliefs in an objective fashion. Just know that the choices you make are the right ones for you. In the long run, the interrelated chain of inspired choices you make will begin to become clearer as you uncover your Self.

As your life changes, it isn't because God's plan for you has changed. It is because your wisdom and understanding of His call have expanded and deepened. This formation is ongoing and, to my knowledge, is never totally achieved in this life. However, it is forever being achieved. As long as you stay firmly in the faith of the Absolute, you will fear no evil. It is only when we step away from absolute faith in God that we are capable of experiencing anxiety and fear about ourselves, our loved ones, and our relationship with God.

There are no complete assurances about anything in this life. That is why faith is so important. Questions such as, "Am I living a spiritual life?" or "Am I doing what God wants me to do?" often surface and cause great concern and sometimes anguish during the spiritual journey. The farther along one is on the spiritual journey, the intensity of the questions fade until ultimately you are One with the question, and it is no longer a question but a fact.

We are reminded in scripture that there are ways to evaluate our progress. Matthew 7:17–20 tells us that a good tree bears good fruit and a bad tree bears bad fruit. Also, a good tree cannot bear bad fruit and a bad tree cannot create good fruit. Our behaviors tell us about the type of fruit we are bearing. Our words are extensions of the condition of our hearts. What are you doing for others? What are we doing to improve ourselves? Are we bearing good fruit in our spiritual lives? The actual behaviors we exhibit tell us if we are living in the Light of God, or if we are living only for our egos. The ego asks, "What is in this for me?" The Self asks, "Do my actions make things better for others?"

Spiritual growth is a mysterious process that we work hard to achieve but we do not control. We must give that control and trust to God. Certain conditions, such as prayer, meditation, contemplation, and inner silence, foster closeness to God.

Do not become preoccupied with progress during your spiritual journey. It is important to stay in the moment and not live in anticipation of what might happen in the future. Remember, movement toward the Self cannot be acquired. It is not "out there" but inside of you. Preoccupation with personal achievement is an attachment and a function of the ego. It is the ego that strives to achieve, outdo others, and be better than the next. The spiritual ego takes us away from God as we become preoccupied with personal accomplishment. The emphasis here is on "me" and not on God. The ego also looks backward to see how much ground has been covered and what is ahead. Remember, we can rest in God and be happy only in the present sense.

To stay on the path is to stay in faith each and every day, even when there appears to be no spiritual movement. It is to stay on the narrow road, even when our everyday spiritual routine seems to disappoint or become tedious. It is to persevere when those around us tell us we are crazy or "going too far out there" and no longer feel comfortable in our presence. Becoming more spiritually oriented people means becoming more aware of our connection to God, of our sure dependence on Him for every breath we take and every thought that comes to mind, always remembering that He is always close at hand, knows us better than we know ourselves, and that we can never be alone.

We can now play hide-and-seek for enjoyment and not out of fear. Everything can be embraced, but the trick is not to attach yourself to anything. It is like a knife going through a well-baked cake; it sticks to nothing. The attachments to worldly things have caused us enough pain and suffering.

The movement of humility and spiritual transformation occur in tandem. Once you have given yourself totally to God, all that God has is yours. You don't have to strive for it, just consent to unconditional love. That is who God is and that is what we are to become in this world. God asks of us, "How can we be of greatest service to the world?" The answer is in the act of our unconditional love to others.

I am often reminded of the part of the Serenity Prayer that is not often quoted. It goes like this:

Living one day at a time;

Enjoying one moment at a time;

Accepting hardship as the pathway to peace.

Taking, as He did, this sinful world as it is, not as

    I would have it.

Trusting that He will make all things right if

    I surrender to His Will;

That I may be reasonably happy in this life,

and supremely happy with Him forever in the next.

Amen.[71]

This prayer asks us for the wisdom and ability to accept what is. In this life, the best thing we can do is to become the best people we can spiritually be. In this way, we lift everyone, as we are all One. The Serenity Prayer also asks us to live life in the moment and trust in and surrender to God. Empty yourself to Him who created you, and He will fill you with His love.

Christ's own words are written out of a very deep level of spiritual consciousness. They are helpful at whatever level they are received. The greater the reader's level of spiritual consciousness, the greater their penetration into the meaning. As faith deepens, the words take on a new meaning. It is the same text; we have just changed. This is life. With disci-

---

[71] http://achievebalance.com/spirit/serenity.htm.

pline, prayer, meditation, and contemplation, we grow into an awareness of this world and the one beyond.

The Last Chapter Is Never Known

There are so many paradoxes in life. We are learning that to become ourselves, we must first lose a part of ourselves called the ego. We are learning that we gain only what we give up. By giving away everything, we gain everything. We must forget ourselves to become truly conscious of who we really are and to know that the best way to love ourselves is by loving others.

As we reach higher and higher spiritual levels in our growth and our climb up the mountain, there is a great demand to start to understand in greater detail this nonlinear world we live in. Without this understanding, the paradoxes make little sense. How in the world can I give it away to keep it?! In a world where everything is "One," when I give love away, it comes right back to me. If I give up everything, I gain everything. Since we are all One, what I give away will always come back to me.

The same thing happens when we look at anger, for example. When I give anger to the world, the world gives it right back to me—or, more appropriately worded, the field of consciousness gives it back to me. Thomas Merton describes this very eloquently when he states, "Man is divided against himself and against God by his own selfishness, which divides him against his brother. This division cannot be healed by a love that places itself only on one side of the rift. Love must reach over to both sides and draw them together. We cannot love ourselves unless we love others, and we cannot love others unless we love ourselves. But a selfish love of ourselves makes us incapable of loving others."[72]

The rift that Merton speaks of is the linear or dual perspective of the world where we see things as good/bad, either/or, and not as "One." All hate, blame, prejudice, and rage come from the dualistic nature of the ego. True joy is derived from love and sacrifice. This is not the language of the ego. This is the language of spiritual transformation and in a deeper sense what the world needs most: love, understanding, and sacrifice.

What does all of this mean? It is all about intention and faith. Our happiness consists of doing the will of God. A good question is, "What is the will of God?" As I understand it, it is to love others as He has loved us through His son Jesus and the Holy Spirit. My intention to love unconditionally has dramatically changed from the days of my youth when I could not even love myself. According to the gospel of Thomas, Jesus said, "One who knows all but is lacking in oneself is utterly lacking."[73] In other words, you can know everything about the material world, but if you do not know your Self, you cannot know God or anyone for that matter. If you fail to recognize the Self in you, you cannot see it in others.

Think of your Divine inheritance. Your gift from God is the

---

[72] Merton, *No Man Is an Island*, xx.
[73] *Book of Thomas* (Boulder, CO: Sounds True, 2006), 13.

life energy breathed into Adam. It is the spirit of His love breathed into us that we have called the Self. Somehow, we must reaffirm this in our lives. This was the gift that Jesus brought to us, a path back to God. This is what every spiritual journey tries to emulate.

When Jesus departed the earth, he sent the Holy Spirit back to help us on this journey. As John relates the words of Jesus, "But the Comforter, the Holy Spirit, whom my Father will send in my name, he will teach you everything, and remind you of everything which I tell you."[74] We are bonded in entirety with Jesus through the Holy Spirit, which is the perfect charity and contemplation of Jesus in our lives. Our nonlinear understanding tells us that consciousness is the Holy Spirit. We are constantly communicating with the Holy Spirit, at least through the right hemisphere of our brains, and the greater the level of spiritual energy we attain, the more "knowingness" we have.

Look back at the journey. As we climb higher and higher up the mountain through spiritual work, there is a growing awareness of God's Law of Charity transmitted to us via the Holy Spirit. We learn these laws as conditions are right for the learning to take place. In order for any of this to happen, we must have as our pure intention to do the will of God. This means we must consent to live as children of God through Divine inheritance. We must accept God's invitation to do so, allowing the Holy Spirit to enter our hearts. Through prayer

---

[74] John 14:26, *Holy Bible*, trans. George M. Lamsa.

and contemplation, we gather the strength to carry out the tasks demanded by the journey. We must carry it out with all of the strength of our desire. If we do so, the Laws of Charity will become intimately known to us and happiness will be ours.

> *Peace rather than dissension*
> *Humility rather than arrogance*
> *Obedience rather than rebellion*
> *Purity and temperance*
> *Simplicity, quietness, and calm*
> *Strength, generosity, and wisdom*
> *Prudence and all-embracing justice*
> *Loving others more than ourselves.*[75]

Humility asks us to be satisfied with simpler goals and accomplishments. If we constantly compare ourselves to narcissistic, egoic, lofty goals, we are living in the illusory future and have become attached to the illusion. It is best to be content in the moment. Just being all right with who you are right now is enough. It was not that long ago that to be all right we had to be bigger, better, and have more than the next. Now, living in the simple grace of God's moment is the task, for there is really nothing else that exists. The rest is all "maya" (illusion). Merton helps when he says, "In order to find God in ourselves, we must stop looking at ourselves, stop checking and verifying ourselves in the mirror of our own futility, and be

---

[75]Merton, *No Man Is an Island*, 61.

content to *be* in Him and to do whatever He wills, according to our limitations, judging our acts not in the light of our own illusions, but in the light of His reality which is all around us in the things and people we live with."[76]

We are to take the message in selfless service to others. There is a potential problem with this, however. For if you are not at peace with yourself and still driven by your ego, even when you try to do the right thing in helping others, you will project your own problems into the action. As always, we have to first find ourselves. It is in the recognition and surrendering to God of our egos that we move closer and closer to Self.

In our work with others, we must be content with the giving of Self without expecting any form of reward. We also need to be able to learn contentment in just living in the moments of our lives without looking back in self-appraisal or looking forward expecting reward. Happiness is found in the moment in the connection with another in need; it is not about special recognition.

You cannot become great in this world until you lose all interest in greatness. There should be no interest in being a great and admired teacher or leader. If through love and integrity our work with others is helpful in getting them on track, we find happiness in their happiness, because it is one and the same.

If we go into helping others with the expectation of grand reward or development of esteem, that is narcissistic and

---

[76] Ibid., 120.

removes us from the Laws of Charity. It is also a manifestation of the ego's value systems for happiness. For example, if I wish to control another because I believe it is the only way he/she can get better, I have lost the understanding that only that person is capable of changing himself/herself.

What is God's idea about how to help? I believe He wants us to rest in Him with the intention of unconditional love toward all we see. To reach this point of unconditional love, one must be fairly high up the mountain to a point where there is no duality, as our egos have led us to believe. At this point, we realize that it is all the same. What we do for others we do for God as well.

In Christian theology, kenosis (the Greek word for "action of emptying/to purge") is the concept of the "self-emptying" of one's will and becoming entirely receptive to God and his perfect will. Mystical theologian Saint John of the Cross's *Dark Night of the Soul* is a particularly eloquent explanation of God's process of transforming the believer into the "likeness of Christ."

The word also refers to an emptying out from the Father to the Son via the Holy Spirit. I believe it also means that we can put ourselves into this formula. Instead of looking to receive, we learn to give all of ourselves, creating an empty vessel that the Holy Spirit will totally fill with God's love. This is the true meaning of joy and happiness. It is about a total giving of oneself.

Other programs for spiritual transformation generally

involve the accumulation of spiritual energy. It is thought that this accumulation allows for a "jump" in spiritual understanding. Kenosis is a much more radical and counterintuitive approach. It essentially involves "giving it away to keep it." During prayer, I might say, "Lord, I empty myself out to you entirely and in my poverty come before you." If I am empty, it creates a larger reservoir for the Holy Spirit.

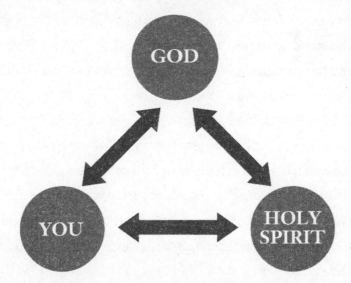

FIGURE 10.1. When we give of ourselves totally, we open ourselves up to receive the Holy Spirit (or Comforter), which is God's gift to us. This is the essence of "giving it away to keep it." The more we empty ourselves, the more room exists for the Holy Spirit to inhabit and shine through. This often starts with a "crack" secondary to an unmanageable situation, such as a chronic illness or a devastating loss.

I always felt I needed to go out into the world and constantly do "good" things in order to win God's love. I know now that I cannot win what I already have. I know now I was trying to say to God, "Look at me; look how hard I am working for you." That was just the ego. I had to learn how wonderful it is to be little. It is humbling to know that I am nothing without God and the Holy Spirit working through me.

We pray and meditate in order to improve our conscious contact with God and to understand what designs He has for us in this world. Remember that "doing nothing" is actually doing something: it is slowing down and intuitively listening to the silence that is God. When you listen for a while, you might find an intuitive sense of awareness arising within. I often find answers in these quiet times.

The Serenity Prayer helps us to understand the fact that we cannot go out and change everything. This evangelical zeal is an egoic illusion. It is the quality of our actions that is important. It is interesting to note that when we go out and try to do too much "to help the world," without quality of action, we will become discouraged. Common sense would say that we would back off and look for guidance at this point. What most often happens is self-talk that goes like this, "You need to do more." Ultimately this will lead to resentment, such as "What's wrong with these people? If they just listened to me, I can help them get well (or save the world)." You can imagine comes next. The individual gets disillusioned and resentful, blaming God and everyone else for their negativity.

Setting aside periods of time to do nothing, pray, meditate, or contemplate the spiritual journey allows for insight. As long as the brain is working too hard and too fast, there is no room for insight. Just rest in the moment and open up your intuitive self-consciousness: the source of all wisdom. Self-knowledge is impossible when our lives are in a frenzy due to chaotic activity. Emptiness and quiet allow for intuitive wisdom.

So where does this leave us in regard to understanding God's will and carrying the Divine message out into the world? The best question to ask is whether there is congruency between your intention and your action. In life, our imperfections will lead us to failure and success, suffering and joy, and emptiness and full-ness. As long as we are on this earth, this will be our itinerary. When we can see all of this as one, it will help us arrive at what our intention is—which is to remove all obstacles to God's love. There is no good or bad action if we are true to our intention.

When we see ourselves as one with God and one with every-thing in creation, we will achieve what Merton describes in his book *No Man Is an Island*: "There, rest and action will not alter-nate, they will be one. Everything will be at once empty and full. But only if we have discovered how to combine emptiness and fullness, good will and indifferent results, mistakes and suc-cesses, work and rest, suffering and joy, in such a way that all things work together for our good and for the glory of God."[77]

We do not need to work twenty-four hours a day to strive to be perfect in our virtue. It is an obstacle to try to be the best in

---

[77] Ibid., 129.

our own eyes and in the eyes of others. It is best just to understand that we miss so much of what is happening in life and that is all right. *We are just trying to master one thing, and that is selfless charity based in humility, trying our best to do what we believe God is asking us to do.* I believe if we pour out everything—all of ourselves—out to God, we will be filled with love and joy beyond our wildest dreams.

Moments of prayer and meditation create the experiences in which the Self moves to the forefront. I believe most will look at the practice of meditation and contemplation and say something like, "Where in the world will I get the time to pray, meditate, and contemplate my relationship to God?" This is very understandable, considering the hectic lifestyles most of us live. It is really nothing but the old argument that states, "I don't have the time to do the things that allow me to grow, be calm, and efficient because I am too busy dealing with the crisis of my unmanageable life." Think about this. Doesn't it make sense that if you approached life in a centered and calm state, there are very few problems to deal with? When we send calmness and serenity to consciousness, this is what comes back to us.

There are so many different ways to pray. We have the Lord's Prayer as a standard. Jesus spoke this prayer when he was asked by His disciples how to pray.

Our Father in heaven, hallowed be thy name.
Thy kingdom come. Thy will be done, as in heaven so on earth.
Give us bread for our needs from day to day.

And forgive us our offenses, as we forgive our offenders.

And do not let us enter into temptation, but deliver us from evil. For thine is the kingdom and the power and the glory forever and ever. Amen.

There is centering prayer (from contemplative Christianity), silent prayer, and these prayers as well:

Prayer of blessing and adoration: The prayer of blessing is man's response to God's gifts: the human heart can in return bless the One who is the source of every blessing.

Prayer of petition: By prayer of petition, we express awareness of our relationship with God. We ask Him for help. For example, *Dear God, please help my son find work in this tough economy.*

Prayer of intercession: The prayer of intercession is a prayer of petition that leads us to pray as Jesus did. He is the one intercessor with the Father on behalf of all men, especially sinners.

Prayer of praise: It lauds God for His own sake and gives Him glory beyond what He does, simply because HE IS.

There are many different prayers and many different ways to pray. From contemplative Christianity, centering prayer is very consistent with the approach taken in this book. Centering prayer sees life as a continuous "dying to self," giving up the smaller self (ego) for the Self. It demands a willingness to let go of desires to create a space for the Divine to work within and heal me. Centering prayer is silent but uses a sacred word to bring you back to the silence that is the first language of God.

Silent prayer is another way to pray and is similar to centering prayer. Centering prayer is a specific technique, whereas silent prayer can involve a number of different techniques, including contemplation—consciously keeping God in mind during the day, for example. By spending time in quiet, we are communicating with God and the Holy Spirit. The silence behind everything is the highest consciousness or God's gift to us: the Holy Spirit. It is a very simple, natural, wordless listening, trusting, and opening yourself to the Divine presence of God.

No matter what style of prayer is preferred, silence and solitude are required. This is best described in the Sermon on the Mount when Jesus says, "And when you pray, do not be like the hypocrites, who like to pray, standing in the synagogues and at the street corners, so that they may be seen by men. Truly, I say to you that they have received their reward. . . . But as for you, when you pray, enter into your inner chamber and lock your door, and pray to your Father who is in secret, and your Father who sees in secret will reward you openly."[78]

Jesus is telling us that prayer is a very personal and private matter between God and ourselves. He is also telling us to be humble and refrain from trying to look good in public, for by

---

[78] Matthew 6:5–6, *Holy Bible,* trans. George M. Lamsa.

doing so, we essentially get no heavenly credit for the act, because we have been rewarded in the human domain. Your inner chamber can also mean deep within yourself where the Self resides.

In early Christianity, some went into the desert to find silence and solitude. The desert stands for outer silence and a place that is deserted, lonely, and quiet, a place where one can go to communicate with God. This calm and silent place allows us to get out of our hectic left-brain hemispheres and into the peace and quiet of the right-brain hemisphere. What is desired is to go beyond concepts, images, and egoic reasoning and thought, thereby entering a deep state of consciousness that is characterized by profound silence and stillness. This is the realm of consciousness or the Holy Spirit. It is often in quiet that we hear the voice of God as an intuitive feeling that gives us an answer or a way to solve whatever problems might be at hand. We receive a blessing in the form of "knowingness."

The first Christian hermits of Syria and Egypt went into the desert in search of God and to face temptation, just as Jesus had done. For them the first step of prayer and meditation was *hesychia* or silence of the heart. To find this place, they used a repetitive prayer called the Jesus Prayer—"Lord Jesus Christ, have mercy on me, a sinner"—which is still used today. This is repeated over and over again, often in rhythm with breathing or the beat of the heart.

Meditation is also practiced in diverse ways. There are focused-attention types of meditations that direct and sustain attention on a selected object such as a mantra (in Hindu and Buddhist religious practice, a sacred word, chant, or sound that is repeated during meditation to facilitate spiritual power and transformation of consciousness) or a spot on the wall. The other general type of meditation is called "open monitoring" or unfocused meditation, and it involves no explicit focus on objects. The most talked about of this type is "mindfulness meditation." Mindfulness is a type of meditation that essentially involves focusing your mind on the present. To be mindful is to be aware of your thoughts and actions in the present, without judging yourself. Research suggests that mindfulness meditation may improve mood, decrease stress, and boost immune function. It is about paying attention to your life as if it really mattered. It is about seeing and appreciating the small things and everyday miracles. There is so much beauty that is missed by not staying in the moment.

The *Twelve Steps and Twelve Traditions* of Alcoholics Anonymous beautifully states the meaning of the words "spiritual transformation" in the following manner:

> *When a man or a woman has a spiritual awakening, the most important meaning of it is that he has now become able to do, feel, and believe that which he could not do before on his unaided strength and resources alone. He has been granted a gift which amounts to a new state of consciousness and being.*

He has been set on a path which tells him he is really going somewhere, that life is not a dead end, not something to be endured or mastered. In a very real sense he has been transformed, because he has laid hold of a source of strength which, in one way or another, he had hitherto denied himself. He finds himself in possession of a degree of honesty, tolerance, unselfishness, peace of mind, and love of which he had thought himself quite incapable. What he has received is a free gift, and yet usually, at least in some small part, he has made himself ready to receive it.[79]

Think back now to the start of this epic climb. Desperate and standing at the bottom of the mountain, unable to even see the top, the aspirant takes those first steps that start the deflation of the ego. Working a program of spiritual transformation using the paths of the heart, mind, and/or action, the ego is deflated and the Self starts to shine through. This happens not by adding anything, but by painstakingly ridding ourselves of character defects such as lust, pride, and envy and replacing them with the spiritual tools of humility, acceptance, forgiveness, surrender, and love.

One way to measure our success is to contemplate the following questions:

Am I truly happy for others when something good happens to them instead of being envious?

Am I someone who can be counted on to complete my commitments in a timely fashion?

---

[79] Twelve Steps and Twelve Traditions (New York: Alcoholics Anonymous World Services, 1952), 106–7.

Am I all right with getting my fair share and nothing more?

Can I be content with a humble lifestyle?

Have I given up my dependence on others for emotional security?

Have I given up my need to control others?

Have I given up blaming others for my shortcomings?

At this point we should be comfortable with our answers and notice a dramatic change in our orientation to the world. Think of the magnitude of change that has taken place. At the start of the climb, I was egotistical, prideful, and arrogant and believed that everyone and everything was out to get me. I believed that nobody had the answer but me. I used resentments to continue my self-destructive behavior because it was always someone else's fault. Look at the dramatic difference in the way I now look at the world: it is a kinder and gentler place than ever before. Dissolution of the ego has liberated me from the illusions that create suffering and has enabled me to see the essence of truth in this world.

Love becomes more natural with the understanding that we are all one and at one with our Creator. Spiritual energy gains momentum, and the ego relinquishes its self-serving and narcissistic self-interests. It is a time defined by the feeling of pervasive joy. At higher levels of spiritual consciousness, we learn to abide in the nonlinear realm and not in the linear dimension. This requires a total change in one's way of being in the world, but it is a change that brings serenity, a tranquil state free of worry or stress. Attaining this level of spiritual consciousness enables us to be emotionally detached from the world in a healthy sense, since we no longer need to control every outcome we encounter. We are able to care deeply for others and the world without letting our emotions rule us.

At this high level of spiritual energy, the spiritual person understands that intention and faith are everything. Pure faith does not worry about what tomorrow might bring and can thus enjoy the moment. Integrity allows one to work with love and selfless service without being attached to the outcome. For example, in twelve-step work with struggling addicts, in love and integrity I do whatever I can to help. However, I cannot control what choices they will make. It is up to them to change their lives; I can't do it for them. While I do all within my power to help, I am not attached to whether or not the intervention succeeds or fails. If the person keeps taking drugs and I somehow feel responsible and obsess about if I should've done something different, the attachment to the outcome is causing me suffering. I also have to understand that I cannot know God's plan and what is best for the other person, nor can I really evaluate the effectiveness of my love and caring about the other. It might ultimately get him/her into recovery quicker—who knows?

This higher level of spiritual consciousness has been described as serenity, where love is a way of being in the world.

As we have been trying to describe the nonlinear realm, words fail to adequately reveal the phenomenon. With this in mind, I will try to give you some indicators of what the experience might be like. Hopefully you will notice some of these subjective qualities in yourself or in others. Qualities that are likely to be noted are:

1. Neurobiological changes with a shift more into the right hemisphere of the brain, leading to a greater appreciation of beauty in all things. Beautiful music, art, and natural scenery, such as forests and shorelines, seem alive and more radiant. It is easy to get lost in the moment, looking at a child or a picture as the "chatter" in your head (left hemisphere) is not constantly distracting.

2. A dramatic shift in what is important to you. Silence and solitude may be cherished. At this stage of being, there is little interest in diversion, as you no longer need to be entertained. The world is funny enough.

3. A total change in one's being, such that the understanding of love becomes obvious. The lower levels of spiritual consciousness are full of emotion (anger, fear, and so on). Higher levels see no need for these emotions, as they are basically useless. Love is not an emotion. It is a way of being in the world, and it is transmitted from the heart.

4. An increased capacity to discern essence. There is an instantaneous understanding of what is at the heart of a situation. You easily see through the "hooks" embedded

in advertising and "games" and "buttons" that once caused you to become emotional. This happens because you have gotten rid of character defects and the ego's programs for happiness. Now, when you see a car advertisement on television that subliminally says to you, "In order to be respected and held in high esteem [remember the affection and esteem program] you need a car like this," you perceive it as petty and ridiculous. All marketing campaigns are geared to leverage the ego. Just think of the journey. It is all about a spiritual transformation where the ego becomes deflated, and humility, integrity, and love become the essence of who you are.

5. A sense of connection to the world and a more holistic view of humanity, which gives you a greater propensity to see the wonder and beauty in life.

6. A greater influence on those around you—not so much for what you say as because of who you are.

7. A "knowingness" concerning some of life's difficult questions, as you attract higher understanding from the field of consciousness.

Spiritual awakening allows a man or woman to be able to do, feel, and believe in that which was impossible to them at lower levels of spiritual consciousness. Earlier, one required the energy of others and the group just to make it from day to day. Now you have a gift that was freely given to you and must be freely given to others. Now you have become a healer.

Personal reflection upon this journey leaves me with the thought that it is a miracle. But then again, miracles happen all of the time. We just have to be tuned in to them. Early in my life, I didn't believe I could ever be happy. I don't even think I knew what happiness was. After a while, I started to interpret happiness as either oblivion or a suspended state of no feeling where somehow the world could not touch me. I have found that it is exactly the opposite. As a part of the whole—the One—I have discovered that it is really all about selfless service.

I am pleased to be connected to you. When love settles into your chest and you put all of your faith in God, wonderful things happen. Incredibly beautiful people enter your life. The essence of the change is love and how love is expressed.

I hope, in some small way, parts of this book have entered your heart, for by becoming that which you truly are, you will elevate everyone around you. The same hand that gives also receives. There is no difference between the two, as we are all One.

Epilogue

Toward the end of 1926, he [Einstein] wrote to Born in words that have become famous through repetition, not least by their author, who liked the phrasing so much he would trot it out at every opportune moment. "Quantum mechanics is very imposing," he told Born. "But an inner voice tells me it is not the real McCoy. The theory delivers a lot but hardly brings us closer to the secret of the Old One. I for one am convinced that He does not throw dice."[80]

---

[80] David Lindley, *Uncertainty* (New York: Anchor Books, 2007), 137.

Whether by simple observation or by more complicated human intent, our connection to the energy around us is relevant to and alters the outcome of events and circumstances. A positive or loving intention will reap a more favorable outcome than will a negative or hateful intention. What we send out to consciousness has a way of coming back to us.

While it is true that subjective experiences cannot be proven per se, there is a "knowingness" that comes from walking through the fire and coming out the other end that is of great, if not greater, value than scientific objectivity. It seems to me that the experience and "knowingness" gained from surviving the hardships of life's journey and arriving at a much higher spiritual plane is an extremely credible platform.

The ego knows of no power greater than itself. It is self-serving and constantly in a battle for survival. It is always fighting or fleeing from some perceived fear. Yet it screams, "Get away from me!" It will do whatever it takes to relieve itself of the misery of life. But it always fails. This self-destructive line of thinking drives us into maladaptive behaviors designed to serve only the ego. To the ego, no one else matters. One cannot see his/her character defects due to the distortion of narcissistic pride.

This obsession to serve the ego underlies all self-destructive behavior. In order for correction to take place, there must be a change in character. There must be a simple but profound return to that which you are: the Self. This is what is called spiritual transformation: to reclaim what you have always had—your soul.

Life places us in positions where there seem to be no answers or options, no door available to us for escape. This end of the line or end of hope is the crucial point. When you are down to nothing, God is up to something on your behalf. There is always an opportunity, a spiritual opportunity. And that is what these moments of despair are all about. When you feel overwhelmed by circumstances, ask, "What is it that is overwhelmed—God or my ego?" Know that God is never overwhelmed. He can carry all of our burdens. It is the ego that is overwhelmed and damaged. When the ego is cracked, there is room for the Holy Spirit to shine through. This energy gives us hope and the ability to push forward.

These moments of darkness of the soul have both yin and yang properties. Yin-yang represents no concrete phenomenon but rather a theoretical method for observing and analyzing phenomena. Yin and yang are a means by which we can observe the two opposite but related principles. The yin of these moments is bleak coldness, stillness, dimness, and inwardly weak movement prior to surrender. The heat, movement, and potent upward and outward direction of surrender with an invitation to the Holy Spirit is the interrelatedness of yang. One can only exist with the other, just like humiliation preceding humility.

Repenting means to change the direction from which you are

looking for happiness. To sin is to miss the mark. We are free to follow the values of our own consciences without fear of upsetting others. Our intention must be pure, and we must follow it. *If you do everything with love and integrity and follow the path laid out in the preceding chapters, happiness and serenity can be yours.* God does not ask you to earn anything; it is there for you when you are ready to learn the tough lessons of this lifetime.

Certain personal characteristics are required for success in your spiritual endeavors. They include the capacity to:

1. Focus single-mindedly on each spiritual lesson;
2. Concentrate on each spiritual lesson with dedication and commitment;
3. Desire to reach a point of serenity and not one of excitement and stimulation;
4. Discover the capacity for radical humility;
5. Perform spiritual work with love and forgiveness, not anger and condemnation.

The road is narrow, and there is not much wiggle room. The integrity of the effort is critical. The process of transformation is a miraculous, life-transforming progression. It is impossible without the direct, active intervention and participation of God. It is an ongoing process. In other words, spiritual conversion is not an event that occurs with no follow-up. Rather, it is a lifelong commitment to spiritual pursuit.

Out of all who start down the narrow road, only a small few

make it to the nonlinear place, which we have referred to as unconditional love. Many more make important, substantial changes in their lives. They climb partway up the mountain. The process of spiritual transformation can catapult one to any place on the mountain. It all depends on the prevailing conditions; honesty, intention, and integrity are only three of these conditions.

Over the years, I have heard many desperate attempts involving individual strategies for conquering the mountain. All such strategies are just mind games played by the ego. Sometimes it takes many failures before a purely virtuous effort is put forth. This effort is no small thing. It takes pure single-mindedness of purpose to keep from stumbling. John McAndrew's lyric from "You Will Always Stumble" speaks of the struggle.

Heard an angel whisper in my ear;
He said, "Don't you worry 'bout it all."
Heard an angel whisper in my ear;
He said, "You're good enough just the way you are."
Then I heard the angel laughing right out loud;
He said, "You will always stumble, you will always fall."[81]

Have you ever trembled in awe as if a current of energy was coursing through your body from your lower back up toward your skull? I am not speaking of the feeling you get when you rise

---

[81] Used by permission of McAndrew Music.

from a chair or bed too fast. The experience of spiritual awe (or numinosum) is the energy of consciousness, or the Holy Spirit. In other spiritual traditions, this energy is called chi or kundalini energy. Have you ever been outside of the dimensions of the linear world or felt uplifted in the presence of another? I believe all of us have had these or similar experiences. For some, these experiences have been more intense than in others.

The term *numinosum* relates to an experience of awe-inspiring mystery or fascination that has the fundamental property of changing how we feel about or think about matters of importance in our lives. The term was coined by Rudolph Otto, who believed that numinous experiences were characteristic of peak moments of spiritual or divine insight and transformation. Carl Jung believed that numinosum provided the primary driving energy for human motivation for personal development and individuation. In his excellent book *The Psychobiology of Gene Expression*, Ernest Rossi hypothesizes that healing or recovery is a process involving numinous experiences leading to altered gene expression, neurogenesis (the generation of neural circuits often called epigenesis, when the alteration comes from the environment), and alteration in level of consciousness. These experiences of awe create within the brain an opportunity for neurobiological change. The precipitating factor for the neural change can be any experience that is perceived by the individual as profound, overwhelming, or overpowering.

Earlier we looked at desire as coming from a sense of internal "lacking." In other words, we believe we are not complete as we are and require something outside of ourselves to become whole. Alcohol, drugs, money, material possessions, sex, and so on were part of the ego's solution to "fill us up." It did not work. But the desire is still there, and now we need to sublimate that energy and put it into working our spiritual programs.

Often a teacher can help. Consider, for example, a wisdom tradition where information and technique are handed down both orally and in the written word from generation to generation. One such tradition is Buddhism. The Buddhist tradition speaks of an "inner teacher." Your inner teacher is your Self that has been clouded by ignorance, distractions, and attachments to life. The job of the "inner teacher" is to work diligently throughout your life to bring you back to that which you are—the Self.

During your early spiritual journey, your inner teacher can become available to you in the form of an "outer teacher." This "outer teacher" is the embodiment of your "inner teacher." When you meet this person, you will have a sense of connection, although you will probably not be able to put words to what you are experiencing. The experience is like looking in a mirror and seeing a person you really want to be. It takes time to find the right person, but whatever time it takes is worth the effort. Look for someone who is humble, experienced in spiritual transformation, accepting of himself/herself and others, and full of gratitude for his/her life blessings. He/She can entrain you in his/her energy and help you along your personal journey.

This book has concerned itself with the trajectory of the changes in spiritual energy as one devotes his/her life to become close to God. The whole journey is based on a simple formula with far-reaching implications. The formula is: *deflate the ego and reveal the Self.*

Wherever we are, we are all on a journey back home. It really comes down to what we are willing to do to get there. How much pain can we welcome? How much about ourselves can we face and endure? Do we have the courage to look at the pettiness of our egos and the people we have hurt? Is it time to come out of hiding? Are we stuck or unwilling? We must always remember that we are not alone.

You have read about life energy—the energy of consciousness—and its importance in the healing process. Over the history of spiritual study, this energy has been called *prana* by the Hindus, *mana* by the Hawaiians, *ka* by the Egyptians, and *thymos* by the Greeks. Hippocrates called it *vis medicatrix naturae*, meaning the "healing power of nature." It is soul, spirit, love, or God, and it is the only energy that can evoke true healing. True healing comes from within, not from outside.

As a spiritual aspirant, a successful journey ahead is contingent upon your understanding that what you are looking for is already inside of you. Once you understand and have faith in that knowledge, the transformational energy can be generated within you, and there will be little or no need to attach yourself to anything external. What a wonderful blessing.

I asked for strength and God gave me difficulties to
    make me strong.

I asked for wisdom and God gave me problems to solve.

I asked for prosperity and God gave me brawn and
    brains to work.

I asked for courage and God gave me dangers to overcome.

I asked for patience and God placed me in situations
    where I was forced to wait.

I asked for love and God gave me troubled people to help.

I asked for favors and God gave me opportunities.

I received nothing I wanted.

I received everything I needed.

My prayers have all been answered.[82]

---

[82] Anonymous. Inspiration Peak website, January 12, 2006, accessed online at weekly message@inspiration peak.com.

Selected Reading

Alcoholics Anonymous. 3rd ed. New York: Alcoholics Anonymous World Services, 1976. Anonymous. *The Cloud of Unknowing.* London: Penguin Books, 2001.

Bourgeault, Cynthia. *The Wisdom Jesus.* Boston: Shambhala, 2008.

Collins, Francis. *The Language of God.* New York: Free Press, 2006.

Epstein, Mark. *Open to Desire.* New York: Gotham Books, 2005.

Fowler, James. *Stages of Faith.* New York: HarperCollins, 1981.

Hawkins, David. *Discovery of the Presence of God.* Sedona, AZ: Veritas, 2006.

———. *The Eye of the I.* Sedona, AZ: Veritas, 2001.

———. *I: Reality and Subjectivity.* Sedona, AZ: Veritas, 2003.

———. *Reality, Spirituality and Modern Man.* Toronto: Axial, 2008.

———. *Transcending the Levels of Consciousness.* Sedona, AZ: Veritas, 2006.

———. *Truth vs. Falsehood.* Toronto: Axial, 2005.

Lamsa, George M., trans. *Holy Bible: From the Ancient Eastern Text.* San Francisco: Harper and Row, 1961.

Keating, Thomas. *Awakenings.* New York: Crossroad, 1990.

———. *The Better Part.* New York: Continuum, 2002.

———. *The Heart of the World.* New York: Crossroad, 1981.

———. *Intimacy with God.* New York: Crossroad, 1995.

———. *Invitation to Love.* New York: Continuum, 1992.

———. *The Mystery of Christ.* New York: Crossroad, 1992.

Kübler-Ross, Elisabeth. *On Life After Death.* Berkeley, CA: Celestial Arts, 1991.

Lindley, David. *Uncertainty.* New York: Anchor Books, 2007.

McTaggart, Lynne. *The Intention Experiment.* New York: Free Press, 2007.

———. *The Field.* New York: HarperCollins, 2008.

Metcalfe, Janet, Margaret Funnell, and Michael S. Gazzaniga. "Right Hemisphere Memory Superiority: Studies of a Split-Brain Patient." *Psychological Science* 6 (3): 157–64.

Merton, Thomas. *A Book of Hours.* Notre Dame, IN: Sorin Books, 2007.

———. *Mystics and Zen Masters.* New York: Farrar, Straus and Giroux, 1961.

———. *No Man Is an Island.* San Diego, CA: Harvest Books, 1955.

Newberg, Andrew. *How God Changes Our Brain.* New York: Ballantine, 2009.

———. *Why We Believe What We Believe.* New York: Free Press, 2006.

Nolan, Albert. *Jesus Before Christianity.* Maryknoll, NY: Orbis Books, 1976.

———. *Jesus Today.* Maryknoll, NY: Orbis Books, 2008.

Nuckols, Cardwell C., and William Chickering. *Healing an Angry Heart.* Deerfield Beach, FL: Health Communications, 1998.

Rossi, Ernest. *The Psychobiology of Gene Expression.* New York: W. W. Norton, 2002.

S. Laura; *12 Steps on Buddha's Path.* Somerville, MA: Wisdom Publications, 2006.

Taylor, Jill. *My Stroke of Insight.* New York: Viking, 2006.

Teilhard de Chardin, Pierre. *The Divine Milieu.* New York: Perennial Classics, 1960.

Trungpa, Chogyam. *The Sanity We Are Born With.* Boston, MA: Shambhala. 2005.

Turk, David J., Todd F. Heatherton, C. Neil McRae, William M. Kelley, and Michael S. Gazzaniga. "Out of Contact, Out of Mind: The Distributed Nature of Self." *Annals of the New York Academy of Sciences* 1001, nos. 65–78 (2003).

Twelve Steps and Twelve Traditions. 37th printing. New York: Alcoholics Anonymous World Services, 2003.

Vyasa. *The Bhagavad Gita.* Ann Arbor, MI: Borders Classics, 2007.

Index